Pearson Revise

Pearson Edexcel GCSE (9–1)

Computer Science

Revision Guide

Series Consultant: Harry Smith

Authors: Cynthia Selby and Ann Weidmann

Also available to support your revision:

Revise GCSE Study Skills Guide   9781292318875

The **Revise GCSE Study Skills Guide** is full of tried-and-trusted hints and tips for how to learn more effectively. It gives you techniques to help you achieve your best – throughout your GCSE studies and beyond!

Revise GCSE Revision Planner   9781292318868

The **Revise GCSE Revision Planner** helps you to plan and organise your time, step-by-step, throughout your GCSE revision. Use this book and wall chart to mastermind your revision.

For the full range of Pearson revision titles across KS2, 11+, KS3, GCSE, Functional Skills, AS/A Level and BTEC visit:

www.pearsonschools.co.uk/revise

Target grade **4-6**

Question difficulty

Look at the Target grade range icon next to each exam-style question. It tells you how difficult the question is.

Published by Pearson Education Limited, 80 Strand, London, WC2R 0RL

www.pearsonschoolsandfecolleges.co.uk

Copies of official specifications for all Pearson qualifications may be found
on the website: qualifications.pearson.com

Text and original illustrations © Pearson Education Limited 2021
Produced by Florence Production Ltd, UK
Typeset and illustrated by Florence Production Ltd, UK
Cover illustration by Pearson Education Ltd

The rights of Cynthia Selby and Ann Weidmann to be identified as authors of this work have been asserted
by them in accordance with the Copyright, Designs and Patents Act 1988.

Content written by David Waller is included.

First published 2021

24 23
10

British Library Cataloguing in Publication Data
A catalogue record for this book is available from the British Library

ISBN 9781292374000

Printed in Great Britain by Bell & Bain Ltd, Glasgow

Picture credits
The publisher would like to thank the following for their kind permission to reproduce their photographs:

(Key: b-bottom; c-centre; l-left; r-right; t-top)

123RF: Kirill Cherezov/123RF 1cr, Dzm1try/123RF 1cl; **Shutterstock**: Vilax/Shutterstock 1l,
Fulop Zsolt/Shutterstock 1r, Iakov Kalinin/Shutterstock 29

All other images © Pearson Education

Notes from the publisher
1. While the publishers have made every attempt to ensure that advice on the qualification and its assessment is
accurate, the official specification and associated assessment guidance materials are the only authoritative source
of information and should always be referred to for definitive guidance.

Pearson examiners have not contributed to any sections in this resource relevant to examination papers for which
they have responsibility.

2. Pearson has robust editorial processes, including answer and fact checks, to ensure the accuracy of the content
in this publication, and every effort is made to ensure this publication is free of errors. We are, however, only
human, and occasionally errors do occur. Pearson is not liable for any misunderstandings that arise as a result of
errors in this publication, but it is our priority to ensure that the content is accurate. If you spot an error, please
do contact us at resourcescorrections@pearson.com so we can make sure it is corrected.

Contents

Pearson Edexcel publishes Sample Assessment Material and the Specification on its website. This is the official content and this book should be used in conjunction with it. The questions have been written to help you practise every topic in the book. Remember: the real exam questions may not look like this.

Using this book

Where are the code files?

 You will see this icon next to some Topic 6 questions. It indicates that a question requires you to edit a Python code file. Python code model answers are provided for most Topic 6 questions.

These files can be found at www.pearsonschools.co.uk/RevCS2021RG.

What notations are used?

Chevrons (< >) are used when the authors need to talk to you about something in Python, but it is not in a Python code file.

For example, <string>.format() is a function call to format a string. The chevrons, < >, are not part of the function call but indicate where an identifier should be provided. The arguments, normally provided inside the brackets in code, are supplied later, because they are not important to the context of the explanation or instruction.

How do topics work together?

Each page covers part of the specification content.

Topic 1 and Topic 6 work together. Topic 1 introduces a concept and Topic 6 shows how to implement it in Python. If you are working in Topic 6 and find you do not recall the terminology or lack some understanding, go back to Topic 1 for a higher-level (more detailed) explanation. Then come back to Topic 6 and try again.

What do the marks mean?

Worked examples and Now try this questions are provided in each section. These questions, in Topics 1 to 5, are similar to the type of questions you will encounter in the Paper 1 exam.

The Worked examples and Now try this questions in Topic 6 are not sufficient to be real exam questions. The marks awarded to them, however, could make up any part of a larger-value exam question.

Are there support materials?

- In the Paper 1 exam, there are no additional materials that you will need.
- In the Paper 2 exam, you will have:
  - a computer workstation with appropriate programming language code editing software and tools, including an IDE you are familiar with, which shows line numbers
  - a 'STUDENT CODING' folder containing code and data files
  - printed and electronic copies of the Programming Language Subset (PLS) document.

Therefore, when revising Topic 6, you should set up the same environment. This will give you the best practice for the actual Paper 2 exam.

Remember, you do not have to learn all of the Python statements off by heart. You can look them up in the PLS, so do practise using it. You can find the PLS at www.pearsonschools.co.uk/RevCS2021RG.

How do I use the Revision Guide?

You may dip in and out of the Revision Guide and Revision Workbook. The pages are independent of one another. However, some of the pages may build on knowledge revised in a previous section. If you need to move between sections, then you will find the 'Links' boxes helpful.

On the other hand, you may want to work from the front to the back of the guide, through all the topics. Because the pages are in the same order as the specification points, you may find that you need to jump forward to revise the points to build on. You will also find the cross references helpful.

Decomposition and abstraction

Decomposition and abstraction are two important computational thinking skills used to analyse a problem, design a solution and refine a solution. The solution is usually an algorithm that can be carried out by a computational device.

Decomposition

Decomposition means **breaking down into smaller parts**. Both problems and solutions can be decomposed into smaller parts.

The decomposed parts of a problem can be tackled independently and treated as smaller problems.

The decomposed parts of a solution can be created or coded separately, then brought back together. For example, a game of snakes and ladders can be decomposed into:

- displaying the board
- rolling the dice
- moving the marker
- taking a ladder
- taking a slide
- checking for a winner.

In code, you might see decompositions as **subprograms** or groupings of code lines; each subprogram or grouping tackles a small problem.

Abstraction

Abstraction is the process of removing or hiding unnecessary details so that you can focus solely on the important points.

In the example of the snakes and ladders game, it is important to know how many squares are on the board and the placement of the snakes and ladders. However, it is not necessary to know the colours of the board or the design for the ladders.

In code, you might see abstraction in the names of variables, data structures or subprograms.

Algorithms

Algorithms provide the **precise instructions** needed to solve a problem. All computer programs are algorithms. An algorithm is a step-by-step procedure for solving a problem or carrying out a task.

Once an algorithm has been written, it can be reused with slight changes for solving similar problems – which is much quicker than starting from scratch each time.

Worked example

Here are four images of seating that will be used in a computer simulation.

Before coding the simulation, a programmer applies abstraction. One feature of seating is colour.

State **three other** features the programmer could include when creating a general model for a seat.

(3 marks)

Other features could be construction materials, the number of wheels, design elements (stripes, dots), width, height.

Number of legs, inside or outside use, capacity.

Now try this

1 Define the term abstraction. **(1 mark)**

2 Give **one** reason for decomposing problems before trying to solve them. **(1 mark)**

Using subprograms

A subprogram is a self-contained block of code that performs a **specific task** within a larger program. Subprograms only need to be written once and can be used as many times as needed within a program or saved in a library and used in other programs.

Pre-existing subprograms

High-level programming languages have a number of ready-made subprograms that perform common tasks, such as handling output to the screen, counting the number of characters in a string and generating random numbers. Some, such as **print()** and **len()**, are built in. Others, such as **random.randint()** and **math.floor()**, are stored in external libraries and must be imported before they can be used.

Abstraction

Using subprograms enables a programmer to design code without getting bogged down in the detail right at the outset. Abstractions allow a programmer to specify what a subprogram must do without worrying about how it will work.

User-defined subprograms

Programmers can also write their own user-defined subprograms to carry out specific functions within their code.

 Links See pages 95 to 96 for information about writing subprograms in Python.

Generalisation

Parameter passing (sending values into a subprogram for it to work on) enables a subprogram to carry out the same task for the different input values passed into it.

Using subprograms

Subprograms are useful to:

- ☑ break down a complex program into a number of smaller, less complicated parts that are easier to code and debug
- ☑ make program logic clearer – for example, a subprogram can be given a meaningful name, describing what it does, and used to replace a block of code
- ☑ make it easier to maintain code – subprograms can be modified or changed without affecting the rest of the program

- ☑ enable code to be used as many times as needed within a program, thus avoiding unnecessary duplication
- ☑ enable code used for common tasks to be stored in libraries and reused in other programs
- ☑ enable a team of programmers to work together on a project at the same time – the programmers can write and debug different subprograms, working in parallel.

Worked example

Target grade 4-6

Explain **two** ways in which using subprograms speeds up program development.

(4 marks)

1 The programmer does not have to write and debug all the code themselves because there are pre-existing built-in and library subprograms they can use to perform common tasks.

2 A team of programmers rather than an individual can work on the program because different subprograms can be allocated to different programmers.

When the command word is 'explain', your response must include a valid point, supported by an expansion or reason. It is a good idea to use 'because' or 'so that' in your answer to show that you are giving a reason. The question assumes that you know what a subprogram is.

Now try this

Target grade 1-3

One reason for using subprograms is to speed up program development.
Explain **one** other reason for using subprograms.

(2 marks)

Algorithms: flowcharts

Algorithms can be displayed as flowcharts. These are translated into program code that can be executed on a machine.

Symbols used in flowcharts

Terminal	Decision/ Selection	Process	Input/Output	Subprogram	Line
Shows start and end of an algorithm. There should be only one start and one end symbol in each flowchart.	Shows yes/no or true/false decisions where there are two possible outcomes.	Shows data processing, e.g. a calculation.	Shows when data is input into or output by the algorithm.	Shows a function or procedure that has its own flowchart.	Shows the flow of the program, i.e. the next instruction to be executed.

Sequence

There are four ways to control the flow of a program. They are known as programming constructs and are sequence, selection, repetition, and iteration. Sequence ensures that commands are executed in the correct order. It is represented in flowcharts by the use of arrows.

Worked example

A program is required to display the sum of two numbers entered by the user.

Draw a flowchart to show the design of the algorithm for the program. **(5 marks)**

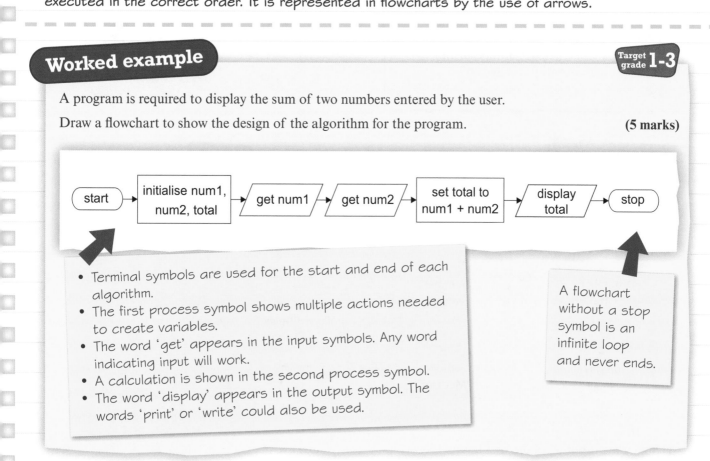

- Terminal symbols are used for the start and end of each algorithm.
- The first process symbol shows multiple actions needed to create variables.
- The word 'get' appears in the input symbols. Any word indicating input will work.
- A calculation is shown in the second process symbol.
- The word 'display' appears in the output symbol. The words 'print' or 'write' could also be used.

A flowchart without a stop symbol is an infinite loop and never ends.

Now try this

Draw a flowchart for an algorithm that greets a user by name. For example, if the user enters the name 'Fred', the algorithm should greet the user with 'Hello, Fred'. **(5 marks)**

Algorithms: selection

Program flow is controlled by sequence, selection, repetition and iteration. **Selection** is used to choose between two or more options. It can be represented in flowcharts, written descriptions of algorithms and program code.

Flowchart

Selection can be represented in flowcharts.

The diamond symbol is used to represent selection.

The words inside the selection symbol should be written as a **question**. The question can have only a **yes/no** or **true/false** answer.

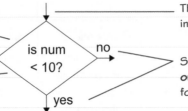

There must be **only one** entry point into the selection symbol.

Selection must have exactly **two** **output** arrows, one for yes and one for no. They must be labelled.

Using selection

You will know you need to use selection when a written description of the algorithm includes choices. These are often expressed using 'if' and 'otherwise'.

If the number is greater than 70, then print 'distinction', otherwise if the number is greater than 50, then print 'pass', otherwise print 'no award'.

Selection in Python

Selection is represented in Python using the **if...elif...else** statement.

```
1    if (number > 70):
2        print ("Distinction")
3    elif (number > 50):
4        print ("Pass")
5    else:
6        print ("No award")
```

elif will appear as an additional selection symbol connected to the 'no' arrow.

Now try this

Target grade **1-3**

Here is part of a flowchart algorithm that uses selection to determine output based on the range of a number.

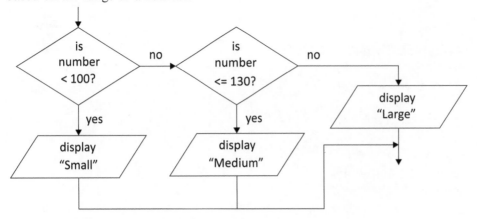

1 State the output when the user inputs 150.
2 State the output when the user inputs 45.
3 State the output when the user inputs 123.
4 State the output when the user inputs 130.

(4 marks)

Computational thinking

Algorithms: repetition

Repetition is the process of repeating a set of instructions until there is a desired outcome. Repetition can be represented in flowcharts, written descriptions of algorithms and program code.

Condition-controlled repetition

Condition-controlled repetition is used when the number of times a loop is executed is not known before the loop is started.

This flowchart shows a loop that continues until the user types in the number 22.

No matter what value 'num' has initially, the user can override it. The number of times the program goes through the loop is totally unpredictable.

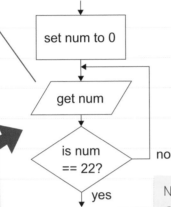

There is no 'loop' flowchart symbol. The loop test goes in a selection symbol.

Count-controlled repetition

Count-controlled repetition is used when the number of times a loop is executed is known before the loop is started.

This flowchart increments a number until it reaches 5.

The number of times through the loop can be calculated, in this case five times in total.

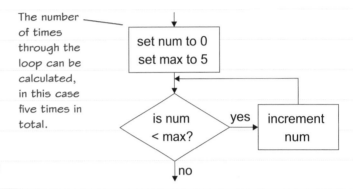

Notice that both flowcharts have a backward pointing arrow going to a selection symbol. That is a loop!

Using repetition

Repetition is needed when a written description of the algorithm includes words such as 'while', 'until', 'go back to', 'for n number of times', or has a set number of repeats.

Until the user types in a choice from the menu, keep showing the menu.

While the temperature is below 0°C, sound the alarm.

Generate 15 random numbers, between 1 and 100.

Repetition in Python

Condition-controlled repetition is implemented using a **while** statement in Python. Count-controlled repetition can be implemented using either a **while** or a **for…in** range() statement.

```
1    num = 0
2    maxim = 5
3
4    while (num != 22):
5        num = int(input("Number: "))
6
7    num = 0
8    for count in range (num, maxim):
9        print (count)
```

Now try this

1 Explain the reason loops do not need dedicated flowchart symbols.   **(2 marks)**

Target grade 7-9

2 Give an example of a word or words, found in a written description, that indicate the need for condition-controlled repetition.   **(1 mark)**

Target grade 1-3

Algorithms: iteration

Iteration is the process of repeating a set of instructions for each item in a data structure. It is also a kind of loop. Iteration can be represented in flowcharts, written descriptions of algorithms and program code.

Flowchart

The use of iteration requires a data structure, for example a string, a one-dimensional data structure or a two-dimensional data structure. The length of the data structure is known before the iteration loop starts. Every item must be processed.

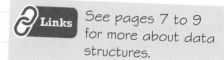 **Links** See pages 7 to 9 for more about data structures.

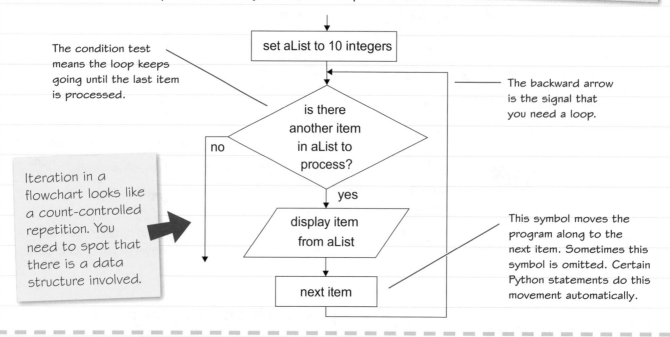

The condition test means the loop keeps going until the last item is processed.

set aList to 10 integers

The backward arrow is the signal that you need a loop.

is there another item in aList to process?

no

Iteration in a flowchart looks like a count-controlled repetition. You need to spot that there is a data structure involved.

yes

display item from aList

This symbol moves the program along to the next item. Sometimes this symbol is omitted. Certain Python statements do this movement automatically.

next item

Using iteration

Iteration is needed when a written description of the algorithm includes words such as 'all', 'for every', 'while not the last' or 'as long as there are more'.

Print every name in the student table.

For every record in the file, read it in and process it.

While there are more characters in the string, display them in upper case.

Iteration in Python

Iteration is represented in Python using the **for…in**, **for…in range()** or the **while** statement.

```
1    word = "Hello"
2    index = 0
3    length = len (word)
4
5    while (index < length):
6        print (word[index])
7        index = index + 1
8
9    for character in word:
10       print (character)
11
12   for index in range (0, length):
13       print (word[index])
```

Now try this

1 Define the term 'iteration'.   **(2 marks)**   Target grade **1-3**

2 State **two** features in a flowchart that indicate iteration is used.   **(2 marks)**   Target grade **4-6**

Variables and constants

Variables and constants are used to store values in algorithms and programs. Variables **can change** while a program is running. Constants **must not change** while the program is running.

Definitions

Both variables and constants represent named locations in memory. These locations hold binary bit patterns that are manipulated by programs.

 Links For a reminder about bit patterns see pages 24 and 25.

Identifiers

Variables and constants have names or **identifiers**. Identifiers describe the data being stored.

- Avoid short identifiers as they do not explain logic very well.
- Use meaningful identifiers to explain logic: theTotal and sumOfAllGrades are much better than t and soag.

Identifiers cannot be the same as reserved words such as print or while.

Variables and constants

Naming conventions

Variables and constant identifiers must be consistent throughout the program.

- Variables are named in camel case, where the first word is lower case.
- Constants are named in all upper case.

The identifier firstName is a variable, whereas the identifier VAT is a constant.

Assignment

Variables and constants are given values using an assignment statement.

- Use the = symbol in program code or flowcharts.
- Use the word SET in flowcharts or written descriptions.

Both firstName = "David" and SET firstName TO "David" give values to identifiers.

Assignments

An assignment is the association of a piece of data with a variable or constant, e.g. SET index TO 0 or index = 0.

Often the assignment is done as an input, e.g. GET name or name = input ("Enter your name").

The value assigned to a variable or constant can be **output** to the user, e.g. OUTPUT name or print (name).

This will output the value stored in the variable name rather than output the word 'name'.

Worked example

Target grade 1-3

Identify the variables that are used in this algorithm and state the purpose of each. **(6 marks)**

```
1   length = float (input ("Length"))
2   width = float (input ("Width:"))
3   area = length * width
4   print (area)
```

The variables are: length, width and area.

The variables length and width store values that are input by the user, and area stores the result of multiplying the length by the width.

Now try this

Target grade 1-3

A student is writing an algorithm that allows a user to input the marks for five tests and then calculates the mean mark.

Identify **two** variables from this scenario that need to be created to store the data in the program. **(2 marks)**

7

Arrays

An array is a data structure, a specialised way of storing data. It is similar to a variable but can store multiple data items, not just one.

Arrays

An array is a data structure that can store multiple items of data, called elements, which are all of the same data type under the same identifier.

Arrays increase the efficiency of a program because if they were not used a separate variable would have to be used, for each element, e.g. name1, name2, name3.

To store four players and their scores in separate arrays, they would be written like this:

```
1    names = ["Alice", "David",
2             "Orla", "Raja"]
3    scores = [10, 13, 17, 20]
```

The elements in an array are enclosed within square brackets [ ] and are separated by commas.

Indexes

An element is an item of data at a particular index.

Index	0	1	2	3	4
Element	red	green	blue	pink	brown

The length of this array is 5 and the elements are at index positions 0 to 4.

The code to traverse this array would be:

```
1    for index in range (len (array)):
2        print (array[index])
```

Inside the computer, strings are stored as an array of individual characters.

Two-dimensional arrays

In a two-dimensional (2D) array there is a second array at each index position of a one-dimensional (1D) array. This array of arrays forms a **matrix**.

Each element has two indices to indicate its position, as shown in the table.

0,0	0,1	0,2	0,3
1,0	1,1	1,2	1,3
2,0	2,1	2,2	2,3

Original 1D array

Each data element has two indices to indicate its position. The two indices describe the **index position**.

There are 3 rows in this array, each having 4 columns of data.

Each element is accessed using the index position, giving row, then column, each in square brackets.

```
1    scores = [[1, 2, 3, 4],
2             [111, 222, 333, 444]]
3    scores[1][3] = 15
```

Worked example

A student recorded their resting pulse rate three times a day (8am, 12.30pm and 8pm) for four days and stored the data in a 2D array.

Day 1	65	73	70
Day 2	69	75	68
Day 3	70	80	65
Day 4	78	79	69

1　State the pulse rate reading for day 3 at 8pm.　**(1 mark)**　`Target grade 1-3`

2　State the pulse rate reading for pulse [1] [0].　**(1 mark)**　`Target grade 1-3`

3　Give the indices for the pulse rate reading for day 4 at 12.30pm.　**(2 marks)**　`Target grade 1-3`

4　Give the output from len (pulse).　**(1 mark)**　`Target grade 4-6`

(1) 65, (2) 69, (3) pulse [3][1], (4) 4

Now try this

`Target grade 1-3`

A student has stored the first name and last name (in that order) of each of their friends in a two-dimensional array named 'friends'.

Write an algorithm, using a written description, that would allow the student to enter a friend's name and check whether that friend is in the array.　**(6 marks)**

Records

A record is a **collection of data objects**. The objects can be of different data types.

Creating a record

In a record, each data element is called a field. Each **field** can be a different data type.

In this example, the fields are a student number (integer), last name (string) and the balance on a dining card (real).

```
student = [3428, "Jones", 12.56]
```

A single record has one dimension.

Setting and accessing each field are done with indexing: `print (student[2])`. This prints the number 12.56.

An array of records

A single record by itself is not very useful, but a collection of records is.

A collection of records is implemented as a nested structure. In this example, there are three rows, one record in each row, with three columns of data.

```
school = [[3428, "Jones", 12.56],
          [1908, "Bradley", 11.75],
          [6231, "Coleman", 5.98]]
```

Setting and accessing each record or each field are done with indexing:

```
print (school[1])
print (school[2][1])
```

This uses one index to print the entire record, [1908, "Bradley", 11.75].

This uses two indices to print 'Coleman', without the quotes. The first index points to the third record, the second index points to the second field within that record.

A collection of records has two dimensions.

Tables

A collection of records can be thought of as a table. Here is a table of car records.

Make	Model	Year	MaxSpeed
"Audi"	"A1"	2015	150
"Hyundai"	"i20"	2013	120
"Jaguar"	"XE"	2016	180
"Renault"	"Megane"	2015	130

The column names are provided here to help you, the reader, but they do not exist inside the data structure. You know this because they have no borders.

Each row is a record, containing all the information about a single car. The items of data are different data types.

Each column is a field, containing the same information about all the cars.

When you need a table of data, you need a two-dimensional data structure of records to store it. If you draw one, make sure to either omit the row and column names or omit their borders.

Now try this

Target grade **1-3**

A table of inventory is shown here.

1 Draw a rectangle around and label a record.

2 Draw an oval around and label a field.

3 Give the number of items of data in this whole data structure.

4 Give the indexes to access the price of 10.00.

(4 marks)

Description	Code	Stock	Price
"Book"	6644	17	27.45
"Poster"	876	67	10.00
"DVD"	7465	135	7.35
"Book"	957	212	5.50

Arithmetic and relational operators

Arithmetic operators are used to **perform calculations** in algorithms and programs. Relational operators are used to **compare** different items of data.

Arithmetic operators

Operator	+	–	*	/	%	//	**
Function	addition	subtraction	multiplication	division	modulus returns the **remainder** after division	integer division returns the **integer part** after division	exponentiation powers of

Relational operators

Operator	==	!=	<	<=	>	>=
Function	equal to	not equal to	less than	less than or equal	greater than	greater than or equal

Order of operations

You need to use the correct order of operations in a calculation (BIDMAS).

- Brackets
- Indices or powers
- Division
- Multiplication
- Addition
- Subtraction

Comparing strings

The relational operators can be used with strings as well as numbers. The strings are compared alphabetically. For example:

D is higher in the alphabet than C so David is greater than Catherine.

'Db' is greater than 'Da'.

Worked example

A chocolate factory packs 20 bars of chocolate into each box. An algorithm stores the number of bars packed per day in a variable named numBars.

Construct an expression to calculate the number of full boxes produced in a day.

(2 marks)

Sample answer

numberBoxes = numBars // 20

> The integer division operator has been used because the calculation is for **whole** boxes.

Now try this

Describe the difference between the arithmetic operators modulus (%) and integer division (//).

(2 marks)

Worked example

Here is an algorithm. State the output when the user enters –12. **(1 mark)**

```
1   num = int (input ("Number: "))
2   if (num > 5):
3       print ("Higher than 5")
4   elif (num < 5):
5       print ("Lower than 5")
6   else:
7       print ("You entered 5")
```

Lower than 5

> Relational operators are used in selection using **if...else** statements to compare the values of variables. The > and < operators have been used but the == operator is not needed as the number must equal 5 if it is neither less than nor greater than 5.

Logical operators

Logical or Boolean operators are used to combine statements or operands, which can be evaluated as true or false.

The AND operator

Using the AND operator ensures that the overall statement is true only if all of the individual statements are true.

```
1    if ((num1 == 3) and
2           (num2 == 6) and
3           (num3 == 10)):
4        result = True
```

For a result to be true they **all** have to be true – they have to be equal to 3, 6 and 10.

The OR operator

Using the OR operator ensures that the overall statement is true if **any** of the individual statements are true.

```
1    if ((num1 == 3) or
2           (num2 == 6) or
3           (num3 == 10)):
4        result = True
```

For a result to be true then any one or all of the statements has to be true, e.g. if num1 == 3, then the overall statement is true even if the other numbers are not 6 and 10.

The NOT operator

The NOT operator is used to reverse the logical state of the other operators.

```
1    if (not ((num1 == 3) or
2           (num2 == 6))):
3        result = True
```

Without the NOT operator, the statement would be true if either num1 == 3 or num2 == 6. Therefore, with the NOT operator, **both** must be false for the overall statement to be true. Note the use of brackets. The statement inside the brackets is evaluated before the condition outside is applied.

Operator precedence

Just like arithmetic operators, logical operators are evaluated in a particular order. From highest to lowest, this is NOT, AND, OR. The order can be changed with the use of brackets.

Worked example

Target grade 7-9

State the output when x = 2, y = 6 and z = 9.
(1 mark)

```
1    if (((x == 3) or (y == 6))
2           and not (z == 9)):
3        print ("Met")
4    else:
5        print ("Not met")
```

The OR statement in brackets is true as y is equal to 6.

But the overall statement is false as z is equal to 9 and it must **NOT** be equal to 9 for the statement to be true.

The output will be 'Not met'.

Now try this

Target grade 4-6

State the output from the worked example when x = 3, y = 5 and z = 7.   **(1 mark)**

Determining correct output

It is often difficult to look at an algorithm produced by another programmer and understand what it does and how it does it.

Dry runs

A dry run is a method used to investigate the functioning of an algorithm. It is a mental or pencil-and-paper run-through of an algorithm that does one step at a time. A dry run can help you to understand an algorithm, and also to find any errors.

Trace tables

While the dry run is being worked through, it is helpful to use a trace table in which to write down the values of each variable, input and output and how they change as the program is running. A trace table has columns for each of the variables and rows for each of the steps in the algorithm.

An algorithm and trace table

Here is an algorithm for a linear search. It outputs Found if a target is in the list. The target value is 13. The trace table below shows the values of the variables during a dry run.

```
1       myList = [3,6,9,13,17,21]
2       found = False
3       length = len (myList)
4       ndx = 0
5       item = int(input("Target?"))
6       while ((ndx < length) and (not found)):
7           if (item == myList[ndx]):
8               found = True
9           ndx = ndx + 1
10      if (found):
11          print ("Found")
12      else:
13          print ("Not found")
```

The variable ndx increments from 0 to 4, as it gets incremented once at the end of every pass of the loop.

The variable item holds 13 throughout the algorithm.

The variable found is False at the start and is changed to True when the target is found.

Columns are used for the variables and output.

item	found	ndx	myList[ndx]	output
13	False	0	3	
13	False	1	6	
13	False	2	9	
13	True	3	13	
13	True	4		Found

The data item at each index position.

The output when the loop finishes.

Here is an algorithm. Complete the trace table to show the execution of the algorithm. **(4 marks)**

```
1   number = 3
2   for index in range (3)
3       number = number + index
4       print (number)
```

Complete the trace table to show the execution of the algorithm. You need not fill in all rows in the table.

number	index	output

Using trace tables

Trace tables have columns for each of the variables and input and output values.

Worked example

Investigate the following algorithm and complete a trace table to show a dry-run execution. **(4 marks)**

```
1    num1 = 2
2    num2 = 3
3    total = num1 + num2
4    while (num1 < total):
5        num1 = num1 + 1
6        num2 = num2 + num1
7    print (num2)
```

total	num1	num2	output

> You will usually be given the trace table in an exam question. You may not need all the rows.

Sample answer

The variable changes for the first three lines of code are done.

total	num1	num2	output
5	2	3	
	3	6	
	4	10	
	5	15	
			15

← num1 (2) is less than total (5), so the loop is entered. The new values are one iteration of the loop.

← num1 (3) is less than total (5), so the loop is executed again.

← num1 (4) is less than total (5), so the loop is executed again.

← num1 (5) is not less than total (5), so the loop is not entered again.

Each row of the table represents one pass through the loop.

Execution continues with the next instruction on line 7, printing the value of num2.

Now try this

Here is an algorithm.

Complete the trace table to show execution of the algorithm. You may not need all the rows. **(6 marks)**

```
1    result = 0
2    total = 0
3    for thePower in range (0, 4):
4        result = 2 ** thePower
5        total = total + result
6        print = (result)
7    print (total)
```

result	total	thePower	output

13

Errors that can occur in programs

An error is a bug in a program that prevents it from executing or causes it to produce an inaccurate or unexpected result.

Syntax errors

Syntax errors occur when the rules of the programming language are not followed, e.g. a command word is misspelled, the punctuation is incorrect or a variable is used in an expression without first being initialised. Syntax errors are the easiest to find and correct because they are flagged up by the interpreter or compiler during translation.

```
    import random
ModuleNotFoundError: No module named
'random'
```

Runtime errors

Runtime errors occur during program execution when the processor is asked to perform an impossible operation, e.g. to divide by zero or open a non-existent file. They usually cause the program to crash.

```
    print (tree (index))
IndexError: list index out of range
```

Logic errors

Logic errors are the hardest to detect. They occur when there is a flaw in the design of a program, which does not prevent it from running but causes it to produce an incorrect or unexpected result.

Finding logic errors

When looking for logic errors, check that:

- variables have been initialised correctly
- the right operator(s) have been used in expressions
- assignment statements are the right way around.

Worked example

Target grade 4-6

A student has written a program to calculate the mean mark and maximum mark for a set of assignments.

Lines 5, 13 and 15 have logic errors.

Construct new lines of code that will correct the errors. **(3 marks)**

Line	Correction
5	numbMarks = O
13	maxMark = mark
15	avgMark = total / numbMarks

```
1    mark = 0
2    total = 0
3    avgMark = 0.0
4    maxMark = 0
5    numbMarks = 1
6    another = "y"
7
8    while (another == "y"):
9        mark = int (input ("Enter mark: "))
10       total = total + mark
11       numbMarks = numbMarks + 1
12       if maxMark < mark:
13           mark = maxMark
14       another = input ("Another? (y/n)")
15   avgMark = total // numbMarks
16   print ("Average", avgMark)
17   print ("Highest", avgMark)
```

Now try this

Target grade 4-6

Describe the types of errors that can be found in algorithms. **(2 marks)**

Linear search

When large amounts of data are searched, it is essential that the searching algorithm is as efficient as possible. Standard search algorithms include **linear** and **binary** searches.

Linear search

A linear search is **sequential**. This algorithm starts at the beginning of the list and moves through item by item until it finds the matching item or reaches the end of the list.

To find the number 37 in a list, a linear search would start at the first entry (20) and simply move to the next item until it finds 37 (or reaches the end of the list).

Indices

0	1	2	3	4	5	6	7	8	
20	35	37	40	45	50	51	55	67	
↑	↑	↑							
≠	≠	=							

The number is found on the third comparison at index 2. Remember: indices start at 0.

Brute force

A linear search is an example of a brute force algorithm. It does not use any specialist techniques, only raw computing power. It is not an efficient method as each search starts at the beginning and keeps going until the item is found or the end of the list is reached.

Program code

```
1    names = ["Francis", "Helen", "Anish", "Mary"]
2    target = "Anish"
3    found = False
4    index = 0
5    length = len (names)
6    while ((not found) and (index < length)):
7        if (target == names[index]):
8            found = True
9        index = index + 1
```

The index < length stops the loop if the end of the list is found.

The **not** found stops the loop if there is a match.

Changing found to **True** indicates a match. The next while will stop the loop.

Worked example

Target grade 4-6

Describe in words an algorithm for carrying out a linear search. **(6 marks)**

1 If the length of the list is zero, stop.

2 Start at the beginning of the list.

3 Compare the list item with the search criterion.

4 If they are the same, then stop.

5 If they are not the same, then move to the next item.

6 Repeat steps 3 to 5 until the end of the list is reached.

It is best to number the steps in case iteration is needed. In this answer, the step numbers are used for the iteration command in step 6.

Remember that the length of the list must be checked to ensure that there are some items to search (step 1).

When coding this algorithm a Boolean flag would be set to 'yes' when the item was found so that no further searching would take place.

Now try this

Target grade 4-6

State **two** conditions that will cause the loop in a linear search to complete. **(2 marks)**

Binary search

A binary search compares the search item with the median item in a list, repeatedly splitting the list in half until the item is found or there are no more items left to search.

Binary search

To use a binary search, the list must have already been sorted into ascending order, either numerically or alphabetically.

A binary search uses a divide-and-conquer strategy to increase its efficiency:

* Select the median.
* Compare it with the search item.
* If the search item is **lower**, discard the median and the **higher items**.
* If the search item is **higher**, discard the median and **lower items**.
* Recalculate the new median.
* Repeat this process until the search item is found (or is not found) in the list.

Median values

✓ The **median** is the middle item in a list. If there is an odd number of items (e.g. 13), then the median is the middle item (e.g. 7th).

✓ If there is an even number of items (e.g. 10), then the median item would be halfway between the 5th and 6th items. As there is no such position as 5.5, the value is truncated to 5 (e.g. 5th position).

✓ Medians, for any size list, are calculated using the formula: median = (length of the list + 1) // 2.

Links Find out more about integer division (//) on page 10.

Worked example

Target grade 4-6

Numbers have been written onto 11 cards that have then been placed face down in ascending order. Show the stages in a binary search to see if the number 28 is on one of the cards. **(4 marks)**

☐ ☐ ☐ ☐ ☐ 36 ☐ ☐ ☐ ☐ ☐

The median card is selected and turned over. The number on the median card is **higher** than the search item, so the sub-list to the **left** is used.

☐ ☐ 17 ☐ ☐

The new median is selected. The number on the median card is **lower** than the search item, so the sub-list to the **right** is used.

29 ☐

The left card is turned over. The new median is higher than the search item but there is no sub-list to the left. This confirms that the search item is not in the list.

The search has confirmed that the number 28 is not on any of the cards.

Now try this

Target grade 7-9

Describe the stages in applying a binary search to the following list to find the number 17.

3, 5, 9, 14, 17, 21, 27, 31, 35, 37, 39, 40, 42. **(4 marks)**

Bubble sort

Data needs to be sorted into order to make it easier to understand and to use. There are many different sorting algorithms. The bubble sort algorithm compares adjacent data items and orders them. Several passes may be needed to sort the whole list.

Order of sorting

Data can be sorted into:

- **ascending** order: 1, 2, 3, 4, 5 or a, b, c, d
- **descending** order: 5, 4, 3, 2, 1 or d, c, b, a

How a bubble sort works

A bubble sort algorithm starts at the beginning of the list and examines the first two items.

1 They are not in the correct order so they are **swapped**.

2 The second and third items are compared. They are in the correct order so they are left in place.

3 The next two items (3 and 6) are compared. These are in the correct order so they are left in place.

4 The next two items (6 and 5) are compared. They are not in the correct order so they are **swapped**.

5 The next two items (6 and 4) are compared. They are not in the correct order so they are **swapped**.

6 When the algorithm reaches the end of the list, the first pass has been completed.

FIRST PASS

2	1	3	6	5	4
1	2	3	6	5	4
1	2	3	6	5	4
1	2	3	6	5	4
1	2	3	5	6	4
1	2	3	5	4	6

SECOND PASS

1	2	3	5	4	6
1	2	3	4	5	6

7 The first, second and third items are in the correct order so they are left in place. The next items (5 and 4) are compared and swapped.

8 When the algorithm reaches the end of the list the second pass has been completed. The algorithm will continue with more passes until no swaps are made. The list will then have been sorted into order.

Worked example

A student has stored the names of some friends in a list.

Complete the table to show each step of a bubble sort to put the names into ascending order. You may not need all the rows in the table. **(5 marks)**

Kai	Camila	Samuel	Muhammad	Mia
Camila	Kai	Samuel	Muhammad	Mia
Camila	Kai	Muhammad	Samuel	Mia
Camila	Kai	Muhammad	Mia	Samuel
Camila	Kai	Mia	Muhammad	Samuel
Camila	Kai	Mia	Muhammad	Samuel

The last pass must be completed, without swaps, to determine that the list is completely sorted.

Now try this

A list is made up of the numbers 4, 1, 2, 6, 3, 5. Give the contents of the list after pass 1 and pass 2 of a bubble sort in ascending order. **(2 marks)**

Merge sort

The merge sort algorithm breaks a list into its component parts and then builds it up again with them in the correct order.

How merge sort works

1 The algorithm breaks the list into two, and then each of these into two, and so on, over and over again, until each list holds only a single value.

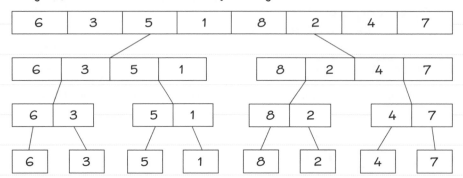

2 The items are then reassembled in the same way but in ascending order.

3 is compared with 6, 5 is compared with 1, 2 is compared with 8, 4 is compared with 7; and they are placed in the correct order.

| 3 | 6 | | 1 | 5 | | 2 | 8 | | 7 | 4 |

3 The leftmost items in each list are the lower items of those lists and the algorithm compares them – in this case, 3 with 1. The 1 is inserted in the new list and the 3 is then compared with the second number of the right-hand list (5). The 3 is inserted and the 5 is compared with the second number of the left-hand list (6). The same method is used for 2, 8, 4, 7 to form two lists.

| 1 | 3 | 5 | 6 | | 2 | 4 | 7 | 8 |

4 The two lists are combined to make a final list in the correct order.

| 1 | 2 | 3 | 4 | 5 | 6 | 7 | 8 |

Worked example

Target grade 7-9

Describe how data is sorted into ascending order using the merge sort algorithm. **(2 marks)**

The list is divided into two repeatedly until each list has only one item. The lists are then progressively merged with the items in ascending order.

For large numbers of items, a merge sort is far more efficient than a bubble sort as the problem is broken down into smaller and smaller problems, which are then easier to solve.

Now try this

Target grade 7-9

A list is made up of the numbers 38, 27, 43, 3, 9, 82, 10.

Draw a diagram to show the steps needed to sort this list into ascending order using a merge sort algorithm.

(6 marks)

Efficiency of algorithms

Choosing the right algorithm to use can depend on many factors, including the type of data, whether the data is sorted already, the time available to write a program and whether the program is a one-off or one that will be used again. The tables below give tips for choosing between algorithms.

Searching algorithms

	Linear search	Binary search
Best case	Search item is the first one in the list.	Search item is at the first median position.
Worst case	Search item is the last in the list or is not in the list at all.	The search item is at the last possible median position.
Choose this for:	✓ An unsorted list. ✓ A short list. ✓ A list that is not going to be searched very often.	✓ A long list. ✓ A list that will be searched often.
Advantages	✓ Linear search algorithms are simple.	✓ Divide and conquer – breaks the list down into smaller lists and performs the same operation on each. ✓ Binary searches execute quickly.
Disadvantages	✗ Brute force – tries out every possibility until a solution is found or all possibilities are exhausted.	✗ Initial list must be sorted. ✗ Binary search algorithms are complex and use recursion (that is, where a function calls itself).

Sorting algorithms

	Bubble sort	Merge sort
Best case	Already sorted list – only one pass through the data is needed.	The number of compares is dependent upon the number of items.
Worst case	Reverse sorted list – one full pass through the list is needed for every item.	
Choose this for:	✓ A list with a smaller number of items.	✓ Long list.
Advantages	✓ A simple algorithm to code. ✓ No extra storage used to make copies of the data.	✓ Divide and conquer approach. ✓ Longer lists add only a little bit more execution time.
Disadvantages	✗ Brute force. ✗ Longer lists use much more time to sort.	✗ Uses additional memory for copies of lists. ✗ The splitting phase must happen, even for very short lists. ✗ Complex algorithm, usually involving recursion.

Now try this

Target grade 7-9

A student has the following names of friends stored in a list.

Ahmad	Ava	Emma	Josiah	Mateo	Maya	Paru	Stephen	Zoey

Show the stages of a binary search to find the name Ava in the above data. **(3 marks)**

Logical operators

Real systems in all computer-aided devices use logic. You can represent logic using statements and truth tables.

 Links For more information about logical operators, see page 11.

AND truth table

A logical expression using AND evaluates to true only if both inputs are true.

This truth table is for the expression P = A AND B.

There is one column for each input and one for the output.

A	B	P
O	O	O
O	1	O
1	O	O
1	1	1

The output shows the result of evaluating the expression for each of the given inputs.

Conventionally, 1 represents TRUE while O represents FALSE. Alternatively, T/F or True/False may be used.

Each column is filled with all possible combinations of values for each input.

OR truth table

A logical expression using OR evaluates to true if either of the inputs is true. This truth table is for the expression P = A OR B.

A	B	P
O	O	O
O	1	1
1	O	1
1	1	1

NOT truth table

A logical expression using NOT inverts the input. This truth table is for the expression P = NOT A.

A	P
O	1
1	O

Worked example

Target grade 4-6

A fire alarm system has a master switch (S) and two sensors (A and B). The fire alarm will sound if any of the sensors are activated but only if the master switch is on.

This behaviour is expressed as:

P = (A OR B) AND S

Complete the truth table for this logic statement. **(4 marks)**

A	B	S	(A OR B)	P
O	O	O	O	O
O	O	1	O	O
O	1	O	1	O
O	1	1	1	1
1	O	O	1	O
1	O	1	1	1
1	1	O	1	O
1	1	1	1	1

Now try this

Target grade 4-6

A seat belt warning in a car (P) must have an output if someone is sitting in the seat but the seat belt has not been secured. There is a pressure sensor in the seat (A) and a sensor (B) in the seat belt mechanism that produces an output when it is fastened.

1 Construct a logic statement to represent the logic of this behaviour, using the symbols P, A and B. **(2 marks)**

2 Construct a truth table for this logic statement. **(3 marks)**

Using binary

Binary is used to represent data and program instructions.

Why binary?

Computer processors contain billions of transistors. These act as switches and only have two states – on and off – similar to a switch on a mains electricity socket.

The two states are represented by 1 (on) and 0 (off) in the binary system. These are called binary digits or bits.

All data is represented in a computer system as patterns of bits.

Binary system

A single bit has only two states 1 and 0, but by combining bits into groups, many unique binary patterns can be produced.

A group of 4 bits is known as a nibble and a group of 8 bits is known as a byte.

All types of data, including program instructions, are represented in a computer system as a sequence of binary patterns.

Representing information

There are only two digits, 1 and 0, but to represent the symbols in text there must be at least 52 separate items of information – 26 lower case and 26 upper case letters.

Then there are the full stops, question marks, etc.

If only two digits are used for graphics then pictures are in black and white, with no other colours or shades.

The bits are combined into groups to represent information – just as letters are combined into words.

Combining bits

If two bits are used to represent each item of information, e.g. a colour, then four colours could be used as there would be four combinations – 00, 01, 10, 11.

The number of items increases by powers of 2, e.g.

2-bits = 2^2 = 4 combinations

3-bits = 2^3 = 8 combinations

4-bits = 2^4 = 16 combinations.

The formula for calculating how many unique binary patterns can be generated by n bits is 2^n, where n is the number of bits.

Place values

Every digit has a place value. In the binary system, place values increase by powers of 2, i.e. the digit on the left has a place value two times higher than the one to the right of it.

Worked example

Target grade 4-6

Write an arithmetic expression to show that 256 different colours can be represented in 8 bits.

(1 mark)

Number of colours = 2^8 = 256 colours.

Now try this

Target grade 4-6

Give **one** reason why a computer doesn't need to know what a binary pattern represents.

(1 mark)

Unsigned integers

You can convert between denary numbers with values from 0 to 255 and 8-bit binary patterns. Denary numbers above 255 require more bits. Denary numbers are also called **decimal numbers**.

Follow the steps in the flowchart to convert a denary number to a binary number.

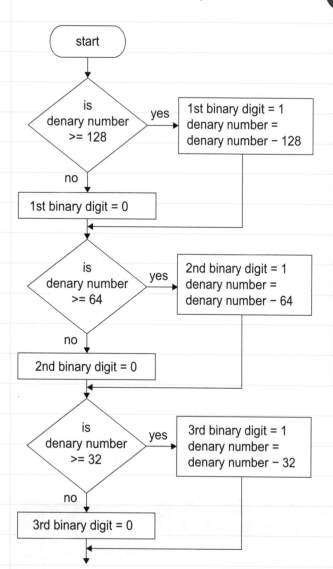

Continue this processing for the 4th to 8th binary digits using the values of 2^4, 2^3, 2^2, 2^1 and 2^0.

Worked example

Convert the denary number 217 into an 8-bit binary number. **(2 marks)**

Compare	Binary digit	Next value
217 > 128	1	217 − 128 = 89
89 > 64	1	89 − 64 = 25
25 < 32	0	25
25 > 16	1	25 − 16 = 9
9 > 8	1	9 − 8 = 1
1 < 4	0	1
1 < 2	0	1
1 ≥ 1	1	

If the number is larger than the place value you are comparing, remember to subtract that place value to get your next starting value. Check that your final number has 8 binary digits.

Converting from binary to denary

To convert from binary to denary, multiply each digit in the binary number by its denary place value and add the results together.

Place values	8	4	2	1
Binary	1	1	0	1
Result of multiply	8	4	0	1
Result of adding		13		

Therefore, the binary pattern 1101 is equivalent to the denary number 13.

Now try this

1 Convert the following denary numbers into 8-bit binary numbers. **(4 marks)**

   203   241   79   100

2 Convert the 8-bit binary pattern 1101 1001 into a denary number. **(2 marks)**

Watch out! If the denary number is less than 128 then the first binary digit will be 0. You have been asked to find an 8-bit binary number, so you must include the leading 0.

Two's complement signed integers

Signed (i.e. positive and negative) numbers can be represented in binary using the **two's complement** form.

Two's complement

Binary two's complement numbers can take a number of forms (e.g. 4-bit pattern, 8-bit pattern, etc.). If the most significant bit (MSB; the leftmost bit) of a two's complement pattern is **1** then the number is negative in value; if it is **0** then the number is positive in value.

To find out how a negative number (e.g. denary –10) would be represented in two's complement notation:

Write out the positive number (+10) in binary:	0000 1010
Flip all the bits – change 1s to 0s and 0s to 1s:	1111 0101
Add 1 (0000 0001) to the result. This gives:	1111 0110
Therefore, –10, in two's complement is	1111 0110

To convert a negative binary number in two's complement to its positive binary equivalent, write it out, flip all the bits and add 1. You can then work out the denary value of the number (see worked example below).

Worked example

Target grade 4-6

Complete the table to show the steps in converting –21 to binary two's complement. **(3 marks)**

+21 in binary	0	0	0	1	0	1	0	1
Flip all the bits	1	1	1	0	1	0	1	0
Add 1	0	0	0	0	0	0	0	1
–21 in two's complement binary	1	1	1	0	1	0	1	1

You should learn the steps for this conversion, as they may not be provided in the question paper.

Worked example

Target grade 4-6

Convert the two's complement 8-bit binary bit pattern 1100 1010 to denary. Show your working. **(4 marks)**

1	1	0	0	1	0	1	0	Original number
0	0	1	1	0	1	0	1	Flip the bits
0	0	0	0	0	0	0	1	Add 1
0	0	1	1	0	1	1	0	Positive binary
128	64	32	16	8	4	2	1	Column headings
32 + 16 + 4 + 2 = 54								Convert binary to denary

Be sure to be clear in your presentation. It is helpful if you annotate your steps as shown.

Therefore, the original bit pattern is the equivalent to denary –54.

Now try this

Target grade 4-6

Complete the table to show how +9 is represented in binary and how –9 is represented in two's complement. **(2 marks)**

+9								
–9								

Binary addition

Binary bit patterns can be manipulated by adding them together. There are some simple rules for adding bit patterns. Remember, the computer does not know whether the patterns represent numbers or not.

Basic rules of binary addition

Binary addition follows the same basic rules as denary addition. Start on the right, move left, and work with two digits at a time.

Apply these rules:

0 + 0 = 0
0 + 1 = 1
1 + 1 = 0 and carry 1

Complete the table to show the result of adding 0011 0010 and 0100 1000.

	0	0	1	1	0	0	1	0
+	0	1	0	0	1	0	0	0
	0	1	1	1	1	0	1	0

Start at the right and add the patterns, remembering to use the basic rules.

Worked example

Give the result of adding 0010 1011 and 0001 0111.

(2 marks)

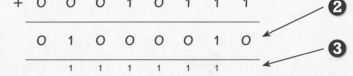

	0	0	1	0	1	0	1	1
+	0	0	0	1	0	1	1	1
	0	1	0	0	0	0	1	0
		1	1	1	1	1	1	

① Write the numbers out one above the other, with an addition sign.

② Start at the right and add the numbers, remembering that this is binary.

③ 1 + 0 = 1, 0 + 0 = 0 but 1 + 1 = 10, so you need to write the 0 and carry the 1 to the left.

Adding negative numbers

Complete the table to calculate adding 10 in denary to −5 in denary using 8-bit notation and two's complement.

If a negative denary number is involved, you use **two's complement** to represent it. That adds another step to do before you can start the adding.

0	0	0	0	1	0	1	0	10
1	1	1	1	1	0	1	1	−5
0	0	0	0	0	1	0	1	Answer

Convert the number 10 to binary.

Convert the number −5 to two's complement. To find out more about two's complement see page 23.

Carry out the rules of addition.

If you want to check your answer, convert it to denary.

Show the result of adding these 8-bit binary numbers. **(2 marks)**

0	1	0	1	0	1	1	1
0	1	1	1	0	1	1	1

Logical and arithmetic shifts

Binary bit patterns are manipulated by shifting their contents. There are some simple rules that relate to these shifts.

Logical shift left

To perform a logical shift left of *n* positions:

1. Move each binary digit n positions left.
2. Discard the leftmost n bits.
3. Fill up the empty spaces on the right with 0s.

Worked example
Target grade 1-3

Give the result of shifting the bit pattern
0001 0100 left by 2 places. **(1 mark)**

Answer: 0101 0000

> Each digit moves 2 places to the left. Any spaces (on the right-hand side) that are created as a result of the left shift are filled with 0s.

Logical shift right

To perform a logical shift right of *n* positions:

1. Shift each binary digit n positions right.
2. Discard the rightmost n bits.
3. Fill up the empty spaces on the left with 0s.

Worked example
Target grade 1-3

Give the result of shifting the bit pattern
1011 1000 right by 3 places. **(1 mark)**

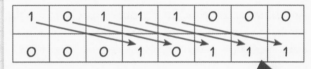

Answer: 0001 0111

> Each digit moves 3 places to the right. Any spaces (on the left-hand side) created as a result of the right shift are filled with 0s.

Arithmetic shift right

This shift is almost the same as the logical shift right, except that the vacant spaces on the left are filled with the value of the original most significant bit (MSB).

Worked example
Target grade 1-3

Give the result of shifting the bit pattern
1110 1011 right by 3 places. **(1 mark)**

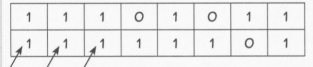

The MSB, value of 1, has been used to fill the vacant places on the left.

Precision of numbers

Shifting patterns that represent numbers can give imprecise results.

The bit pattern 0000 0100 (4) shifted left by 1 place is 0000 1000 (8). This makes sense, as 8 is twice 4. However, the bit pattern 1000 0100 (−124) shifted left by 1 place is 0000 1000 (8).

The bit pattern 0000 0100 (4) shifted right by 1 place is 0000 0010 (2). This makes sense, as 2 is half of 4. However, the bit pattern 0000 0111 (7) shifted right by 1 place is 0000 0011 (3).

> An **arithmetic shift left** is the same as a logical shift left, as the MSB is shifted left out of the pattern. Fill the vacant positions on the right with 0s.

Now try this
Target grade 1-3

For each of the following, give the result of applying:

1 A logical shift left, 2 places, to the 8-bit binary pattern 0001 0100. **(1 mark)**

2 A logical shift right, 3 places, to the 8-bit binary pattern 1011 1000. **(1 mark)**

3 An arithmetic shift right, 1 place, to the 8-bit binary pattern 1000 1000. **(1 mark)**

Overflow

An overflow occurs when an operation produces a result that requires more bits to store it than are available in the computer.

Addition overflow

Adding two 8-bit binary patterns can generate an overflow error.

```
  1  0  1  1  0  1  0  1
  1  1  0  0  1  1  1  1
_____
1  1  0  0  0  0  1  0  0
```

Remember: binary patterns are stored in registers of a fixed length. There is no extra space to store the overflow bit.

The result cannot be represented by an 8-bit number. A 9th bit is required – this is the overflow. Programmers must make allowances for this to prevent serious errors or disasters.

Consequences of overflow errors

Any time an operation produces an inaccurate result, program errors may occur. Programs may crash or produce unreliable or incorrect results.

High-level language programmers do not need to worry about overflow errors, as the language translator has mechanisms for handling and reporting them when they occur.

Worked example

Target grade 4-6

Calculate the result of adding the two 8-bit binary numbers 0101 0110 and 1110 1000. **(2 marks)**

```
    0  1  0  1  0  1  1  0
    1  1  1  0  1  0  0  0
  _____
1 | 0  0  1  1  1  1  1  0
  __|
  | 1
```

1. Write the numbers out one above the other.
2. Draw borders to help you, especially the vertical one to show the 8-bit limit on the left.
3. Carry out the addition as normal.
4. It is a good idea to show the carries as this will help you with the addition.

The vertical bar separating the 8th and 9th bit shows that the overflow is not part of the answer. Another way of showing this is (1) 0011 1110

Registers hold the bit patterns that are added. They are of a fixed width. If the original patterns are 8 bits, then the result is 8 bits. No new bits can be added to make a register bigger.

Now try this

Target grade 4-6

1. Explain one reason why the result of adding two 16-bit binary patterns together must be 16 bits in length. **(2 marks)**

2. Complete the table on the right to show the result of adding the two 8-bit binary numbers 1101 0011 and 1101 1010. **(2 marks)**

```
1  1  0  1  0  0  1  1
1  1  0  1  1  0  1  0
_____
```

Hexadecimal

Hexadecimal numbers are used to help programmers manipulate large binary numbers because computers do not use hexadecimal numbers – they only understand binary. Hexadecimal numbers represent long binary numbers using fewer digits, as every eight digits of a binary number can be represented by two hexadecimal digits.

Worked example

Target grade 1-3

Convert the binary number 1011 0011 into a hexadecimal number.   **(2 marks)**

1011 0011

Place value   1011 → ← 0011

1	0	1	1
8	4	2	1
8	0	2	1

= 8 + 2 + 1 = 11

0	0	1	1
8	4	2	1
0	0	2	1

= 2 + 1 = 3

11 in hexadecimal is B
3 in hexadecimal is 3

Therefore the hexadecimal number is B3

Converting binary to hexadecimal

1 Split the 8-bit byte into two 4-bit nibbles.

2 Convert the bits in each nibble into denary numbers using the place values.

3 Add these together to give the hexadecimal.

Converting hexadecimal to binary

Converting hexadecimal to binary reverses the process of converting binary to a hexadecimal number.

1 Each hexadecimal digit is converted to denary.

2 Each denary number is converted into a nibble.

3 The nibbles are combined to give the binary number.

Worked example

Target grade 1-3

Convert the hexadecimal C3 to binary.   **(2 marks)**

C3

12 ← ← 3

8	4	2	1
1	1	0	0

8	4	2	1
0	0	1	1

1100 0011

Use of hexadecimal

- ✓ Hexadecimal notation is used to help humans cope with long strings of binary digits – they are much shorter in hexadecimal.
- ✓ When a computer malfunctions, error code numbers are usually given in hexadecimal.
- ✓ Hexadecimal is also used to represent numerical values in assembly language.

True colour

True colour uses 24 bits to code every available colour variation: 2^{24} = 16 777 216.

Each one is represented by three 8-bit numbers that can be simplified to three 2-digit hexadecimal ones, e.g. 1100 0110 0011 0000 1111 0100 can be represented as C630F4. It is far easier to remember and enter the six digits of the hexadecimal number than the 24 digits of the binary number.

#FF0000	#FFA500	#FFFF00	#00FF00	#00FFFF	#FF00FF
HEX

Worked example

Target grade 1-3

Convert the 8-bit binary number 1011 0111 to hexadecimal.   **(1 mark)**

1011 = 11 in denary
0111 = 7 in denary
    = B7 in hexadecimal

Now try this

Target grade 1-3

Convert the hexadecimal number E9 to 8-bit binary.   **(1 mark)**

Characters

Computers represent text characters, numbers and symbols in binary as strings of 1s and 0s.

ASCII code

- Text and characters are represented by the ASCII code (American Standard Code for Information Interchange).
- ASCII is a **7-bit code**. There are **128** (2^7) code sequences representing English characters and control actions such as SPACE and SHIFT.

> The ASCII code for the letter C is **100 0011** (67 in denary); and for the control action SPACE is **010 0000** (32 in denary).

- The **character set** is the list of binary codes that can be recognised by the computer hardware and software.

ASCII code groups

ASCII codes are grouped according to function.

0–32	Control codes, e.g. SHIFT, SPACE
33–47	Symbols, e.g. (, !, *
48–57	Digits 0 to 9
58–64	Symbols, e.g. @, <, >
65–90	Upper-case characters, e.g. A, Z
91–96	Symbols, e.g. [, \,]
97–122	Lower-case characters, e.g. a, z
123–127	Symbols, e.g. {, DEL, }

ASCII codes in Python

In Python, the function ord( ) returns the ASCII code (in denary) for a character and the function chr( ) returns the character for a denary code.

```
1    code = ord ("c")          Returns 99
2    char = chr (100)          Returns "d"
```

Finding the ASCII code

As the upper-case and lower-case letters are consecutive, if one is known then others can be calculated.

For example, if you know that the code for the letter 'a' is 97 in denary then the code for the letter 'c' must be 99.

Also if you know that 83 is the code for an upper-case S then 87 must be the code for upper-case W.

Worked example

Target grade **4-6**

Here is a variable definition: myString = **"Once upon a time."**

1 Write a program to print the ASCII codes of each of the characters in myString.   **(2 marks)**

2 The character at index [2] returns the number 99 and index [3] returns 101. State the number that will be returned at index [8].   **(1 mark)**

Sample answer

```
1    for index in range (len(myString)):
         print (ord (myString[index]))
2    110
```

> Lower-case characters are in the range 97 to 122. The letter 'c', at index [2], is 99 and 'e' is 101. Therefore, the letter 'n' will be 110 as 'n' is nine places further along in the alphabet than 'e'. Do not forget to count the spaces!

Now try this

Target grade **1-3**

The ASCII code for character 'C' is 67.

Give the ASCII code for the character 'M'.   **(1 mark)**

Bitmap images

In a computer all images are represented as strings of 1s and 0s.

Pixels

A digital image is composed of many small points of colour. Each one is called a **pixel** (short for **picture element**). Each pixel has its own individual colour. The greater the number of pixels, the greater the detail in the picture.

Image size

The size of an image is given as the number of pixels in its width (W) and height (H), e.g. 3000 × 1000.

Colour depth

Colour depth is the number of bits used to encode the colour of each pixel.

The more bits used to encode the colour, the greater the number of actual colours that can be represented in the image so that it is more detailed.

Number of bits	Number of colours
1	2 (2^1)
8	256 (2^8)
24	16 777 216 (2^{24})

Modern cameras and smartphones produce images with a colour depth of 24 bits.

Image file size

- ☑ The size of an image file in bits depends on image size and colour depth.
- ☑ The file size in bits can be calculated using the following formula:

$$\underset{\text{width}}{W} \times \underset{}{H} \times \underset{\text{colour depth}}{D} \quad \overset{\text{height}}{}$$

- ☑ The better the image quality, the larger the file size. Large file sizes can be a problem if they are being transferred electronically or if storage space is limited.

Resolution

The resolution describes the number of pixels per inch when the image is displayed, e.g. on a monitor or on paper.

Look how sharp the small image is and how blurred it becomes when enlarged because it has a lower resolution. Individual pixels are visible.

When the small image is enlarged to cover a larger area it is less sharp as there are now fewer pixels per unit area and each individual pixel has to be enlarged. It is said to have a lower **resolution** – resolution describes the number of pixels per unit area.

If an image is enlarged too much then it becomes **pixelated** and individual pixels can be seen.

Worked example   Target grade 4-6

An image with 24-bit colour depth has the dimensions 410 × 270 pixels.

Construct an expression to calculate the size of the image file (MiB). You do not need to carry out the calculation. **(2 marks)**

(410 × 270 × 24) ÷ (8 × 1024 × 1024)

Now try this   Target grade 4-6

Describe the factors that affect the quality of a digital image. **(4 marks)**

The file size of the image in bits is 410 × 270 × 24. Dividing by 8 × 1024 × 1024 converts the file size to **mebibytes**. See page 32.

Analogue sound

Sounds can be represented in digital form as streams of 1s and 0s. Sound is caused by vibrations travelling through a medium such as air, water or metal. Sound recordings convert the changes in air pressure into voltage changes. These are **analogue recordings**.

Sound sampling

Samples of a sound wave are taken at regular fixed intervals. This is called the **sample interval**. The number of samples over a given time period is the **sample rate**. A high sample rate gives a more accurate reproduction of the sound's analogue waveform.

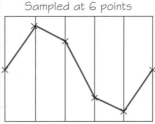

Original waveform · Sampled at 10 points · Sampled at 6 points · Sampled at 2 points

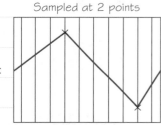

> The loss in quality is represented here by the shape of the waveform – the diagram with 10 samples is much closer to the original shape than the one with only 2 samples.

For CDs, a sample rate of 44 100 per second (44.1 kHz) is used. A sample rate of 96 000 Hz is used for Blu-ray audio.

> 1 hertz (Hz) = 1 cycle per second,
> 1 kHz = 1 kilohertz = 1000 Hz.

CDs are recorded in stereo and so have two channels. Therefore the total file size will be doubled.

Digital sound recording

Transistors are either on or off, and cannot continuously reproduce analogue changes. Instead, digital recordings use snapshots of the sound at regular fixed intervals and then play them back one after the other. These snapshots are called **samples**.

A digital sound recording is like an animated film that consists of many still images with tiny differences between them. When played back quickly the film creates an illusion of movement.

Bit depth

✓ The bit depth describes the number of bits used to encode each sample.

✓ Using 8 bits allows 256 gradations of volume; 16 bits allows 65 536 and 24 bits allows for 16.7 million.

Audio file sizes

You can calculate the size of an audio file using the equation:

$$\text{file size (bits)} = \text{sample rate} \times \text{bit depth} \times \text{recording length (seconds)}$$

If the file size is a limiting factor, then a lower sample rate and bit depth have to be used. This reduces the accuracy or fidelity of the digital representation of the analogue signal.

> Fidelity means how accurately a copy matches the original.

Worked example

Target grade **4-6**

Construct an expression to calculate the size in mebibytes of a digital audio file of 3 minutes duration with a sample rate of 44.1 kHz and a bit depth of 16 bits. **(2 marks)**

File size (bits) = sample rate × bit depth × recording length (seconds)

(44 100 × 16 × 180) ÷ (8 × 1024 × 1024) MiB

Now try this

Target grade **4-6**

1 An analogue signal is never fully reproducible in a digital format.

   Explain **one** reason why this statement is true. **(2 marks)**

2 Construct an expression to calculate the file size in mebibytes of a stereo audio file if the duration is 2 minutes 30 seconds and the sample rate is 44.1 kHz with a bit depth of 16 bits. **(2 marks)**

Limitations of binary representation of data

The number of bits available to store data limits the number and range of values that can be represented by those bits.

Number of values

The number of different binary patterns that can be represented using a known number of bits is calculated by the formula 2^n, where n is the number of bits.

Bits	Calculation	Number of patterns
1	2^1	2
2	2^2	4
8	2^8	256
16	2^{16}	65 536

The more bits you have available to store a pattern, the wider the range of values the pattern can represent.

Four-bit binary will have patterns of 0000, 0001, ... 1110, 1111. There are 16 distinct patterns. Eight-bit binary will have patterns of 00000000, 00000001, 00000010, ... 11111110, 11111111. There are 256 distinct patterns.

Unsigned and signed integers

If the binary bit patterns are interpreted as **unsigned integers**, then 4 bits can represent the numbers 0 to 15 and 8 bits can represent the numbers 0 to 255.

If the binary bit patterns are interpreted as two's complement **signed integers**, 4 bits can represent the numbers -8 to +7, and 8 bits the numbers -128 to +127.

Characters

The 7-bit ASCII character set gives 128 (2^7) different patterns. This is enough to represent English letters (both upper- and lower-case), digits and some control characters. To represent other alphabets, such as Kanji and Cyrillic, more bits are required.

The Unicode character set was introduced to encode text and symbols not in the original ASCII set. It uses more bits to store characters than ASCII.

Various types of encoding allow for over 140 000 different characters.

You might have seen these characters as mathematical symbols or smiley faces: ÷ ☺

Bitmap images

Colour depth is the number of bits used to represent the colour of each pixel in an image.

If colour depth is 4 bits, then 16 colours can be used. Every pixel would be one of only 16 colours.

Increasing the number of bits in the colour depth to 16, gives 2^{16} or 65 536 possible colours.

Increasing the colour depth also increases the amount of storage required for the image file.

Sounds

Bit depth is the number of bits used to represent a single sample of audio.

If the bit depth is 16 bits, then one of 2^{16} distinct values can be used for each sample.

Increasing the bit depth to 24 bits gives a wider range of values.

Now try this

Target grade **4-6**

Explain **one** reason that a 5-bit colour depth is needed to store 24 colours in an image.

(2 marks)

Binary units of measurement

All data processed by a computer must be converted into binary format, a sequence of 1s and 0s.

Units

One unit, either a 1 or a 0, is called a **bit** – short for **binary digit**. More than one digit is needed to represent an item of data (such as a letter).

Bits are organised into groups:

- 4 bits = 1 nibble
- 8 bits = 1 byte

Conventions

Until recently, standard decimal prefixes – kilo, mega, giga, etc. – have been used to represent binary multiples. This has caused some confusion. To address this, the International Electrotechnical Commission (IEC) has produced a set of **binary prefixes** to represent binary multiples. These are the units of measurement to be used for data storage.

Groups of bytes

Bytes are grouped into the larger units shown below.

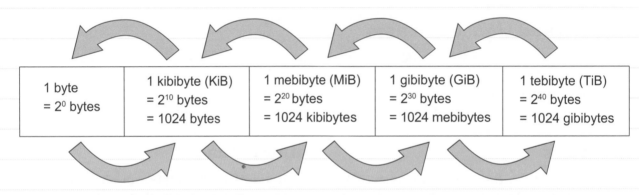

| 1 byte $= 2^0$ bytes | 1 kibibyte (KiB) $= 2^{10}$ bytes $= 1024$ bytes | 1 mebibyte (MiB) $= 2^{20}$ bytes $= 1024$ kibibytes | 1 gibibyte (GiB) $= 2^{30}$ bytes $= 1024$ mebibytes | 1 tebibyte (TiB) $= 2^{40}$ bytes $= 1024$ gibibytes |

1024 is called a binary prefix for converting between units.

Multiply by 1024 to convert a larger unit into a smaller unit. Divide by 1024 to convert a smaller unit into a larger unit. For example, to convert gibibytes into bytes multiply by 1024 × 1024 × 1024. To convert bytes into mebibytes divide by 1024 × 1024.

Worked example

Target grade 4-6

A flash drive (USB stick) has a storage capacity of 32 GiB.

Construct an expression to show the capacity of the drive in bits. You do not have to do the calculation. **(2 marks)**

32 × 1024 × 1024 × 1024 × 8

Now try this

Target grade 4-6

Ann needs to convert a file size from mebibytes (MiB) to gibibytes (GiB).

Describe how she could convert 4096 MiB to GiB. **(2 marks)**

Data compression

The sizes of large files can be reduced using compression algorithms that repackage the data or remove some of it.

	Lossless compression	Lossy compression
What it does	• Reduces file sizes without deleting any data. • Nothing is lost.	• Reduces file size by deleting some data. • The original can never be reconstituted – it has been irreversibly changed.
How it compresses	• Looks for redundancy where the same data is stored many times and groups this data into one reference.	• In image files, algorithms analyse the image and find areas where there are only slight differences. These are given the same value and the file can be rewritten using fewer bits. • In digital sound recordings very small variations in frequency, tone and volume are removed to reduce the file size as the human ear cannot detect these small differences.
Uses	• Text files • Graphic files with a low colour depth	• Image files • Digital sound recordings
Less successful uses	• Audio files • 24-bit colour files	• Text files • Executable software
Examples	• Compressed text files • GIF and PNG image files • FLAC and ALAC audio files	• MP3 audio files • JPG image files

These audio formats can reduce the size of an uncompressed file by about 50% and are becoming more popular on downloading websites for people who prioritise sound quality over small file size.

An MP3 file is usually about one tenth of the size of an uncompressed file, so more files can be stored on discs and SD cards.

The need for compression

Billions of video, audio, multimedia and image files are uploaded and downloaded each day. Smaller file sizes make file transfer more efficient and reduce the requirements for storage space.

The advantages of file compression are:

• less internet bandwidth is used when files are downloaded/uploaded
• transfer time is faster
• less storage space is needed
• smaller files reduce congestion on the internet
• audio and video files can be streamed.

Worked example

Target grade 4-6

Describe the difference between lossy and lossless compression and give an example where each would be used. **(4 marks)**

In lossy compression, when the compressed data is uncompressed again, it is not exactly the same as the original but the difference is so small that it cannot normally be noticed, e.g. for audio files (MP3) and digital image files (JPG).

In lossless compression, when the compressed data is uncompressed, it is restored completely to the original file, e.g. compressed text files.

Remember to give an example where each would be used.

Now try this

Target grade 4-6

1   Explain the importance of compressing files when they are transmitted over the internet. **(2 marks)**

2   Explain the best type of compression to use on a Python program code file that is being sent by email from a student to a teacher. **(2 marks)**

The stored program concept

The stored program concept was the brainchild of Alan Turing and John von Neumann in the 1940s. They wanted to make a computer that was easy and quick to reprogram so that it could carry out a variety of tasks. Previously, computing machines were built to perform just one job.

Programmable computers

The term **computer architecture** refers to the structure of a computer system – the hardware components it has and how they work together to execute programs.

Von Neumann devised a new computer architecture for a programmable machine.

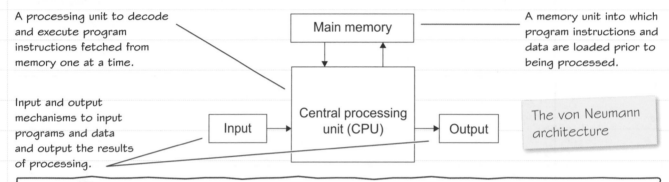

A processing unit to decode and execute program instructions fetched from memory one at a time.

A memory unit into which program instructions and data are loaded prior to being processed.

Input and output mechanisms to input programs and data and output the results of processing.

The von Neumann architecture

Being able to store programs in memory was a major breakthrough. It enabled computers to be general purpose machines capable of carrying out lots of different tasks.

Although invented in the 1940s, the von Neumann architecture is still the basis for the design of most modern computers.

Key facts about main memory

- It is **short-term**, working memory. It only holds the program instructions and data that the CPU is currently using. The contents of main memory are continually changing.
- It consists of a **collection of storage locations**, each with its own unique address. A storage location can hold a program instruction or an item of data.
- It is often referred to as **RAM** – short for random access memory – because storage

locations can be read from and written to in any order.
- It is classed as **primary storage** because the CPU has fast, direct access to it.
- It is **volatile**. It needs power to retain its contents. When the computer is switched off, its main memory is completely wiped.
- Modern laptops, tablets and phones typically have between 4 and 32 GiB of RAM. This enables them to store several programs in memory at the same time.

Worked example

Target grade **7-9**

Explain **one** reason why the stored program concept enabled computers to become general purpose machines capable of performing a variety of different tasks. **(2 marks)**

Computers could then be reprogrammed to carry out different tasks, because they were able to store program instructions and data in memory.

Now try this

Target grade **4-6**

Describe how the CPU and main memory work together to run programs. **(4 marks)**

The central processing unit (CPU)

The CPU is the hardware component that decodes and executes program instructions.

Components of the CPU

Three buses work together to transfer data between the CPU, main memory and input/output devices such as the keyboard and screen.

Fetches program instructions from main memory one at a time, decodes them and directs the operations of the other parts of the system to execute them.

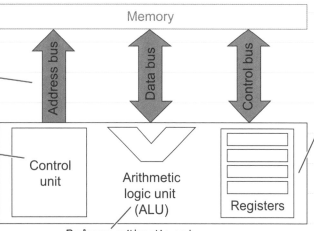

Direct-access storage for instructions, intermediate results and data within the CPU. Some are general purpose. Others, such as the Program counter and the Instruction register, have specific functions.

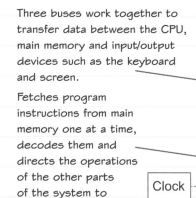

Synchronises the actions of the CPU.

Performs arithmetic and logic operations on data.

The clock

The CPU's clock is a tiny quartz crystal that vibrates at a constant rate. Each 'tick' of the clock triggers the CPU to carry out one action.

The clock's speed is measured in cycles per second: 1 hertz = 1 cycle per second. Modern CPUs have clock speeds of around 3 gigahertz (GHz).

Every CPU requires a fixed number of clock cycles to execute an instruction. The higher the clock speed, the more instructions that can be executed per second. Some CPUs need two cycles to fetch an instruction. One to get the instruction and the second to get the data needed to carry it out. Others fetch both in one cycle.

Buses

A bus is a collection of wires that is used to transfer data between components of a computer system. The CPU uses three buses:

- The **control bus** carries **signals** between the CPU and other parts of the computer system.
- The **address bus** holds the address of the memory location that the CPU will read from or write to. The number of wires in the address bus (its **bandwidth**) determines how much addressable memory there is.
- The **data bus** transfers program instructions and data between memory and the CPU.

Buses may be **unidirectional** (one way) or **bidirectional** (two ways).

Worked example

Target grade 7-9

Describe how the bandwidth of the address bus determines the size of the memory that a CPU can use. **(3 marks)**

Each memory location has a unique binary address. Each wire in the address bus represents one bit of the address, so the number of wires in the address bus determines how many unique addresses can be generated, e.g. a 32-bit address bus can represent 2^{32} different memory addresses.

Now try this

Target grade 7-9

Describe **one** reason the data bus needs to be bi-directional. **(2 marks)**

The fetch-decode-execute cycle

The fetch-decode-execute cycle is the sequence of steps carried out repeatedly by the CPU when a program is being executed. Instructions are fetched one at a time from memory into the CPU, where they are decoded and executed. Modern CPUs carry out billions of cycles per second.

The fetch stage

To fetch an instruction.

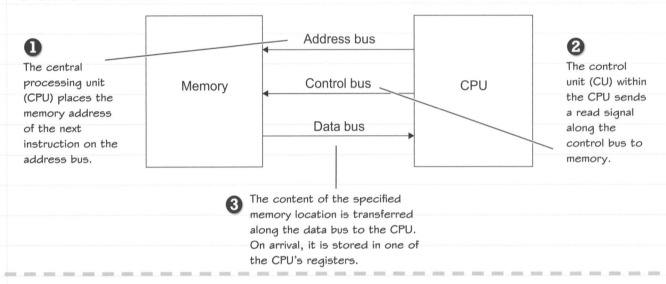

❶ The central processing unit (CPU) places the memory address of the next instruction on the address bus.

Memory

Address bus

Control bus

Data bus

CPU

❷ The control unit (CU) within the CPU sends a read signal along the control bus to memory.

❸ The content of the specified memory location is transferred along the data bus to the CPU. On arrival, it is stored in one of the CPU's registers.

The decode stage

Next, the control unit looks up the instruction in the CPU's instruction set. Every CPU has its own unique instruction set – a list of all the operations that it can carry out.

The execute stage

Finally, the control unit coordinates the actions of the other components of the CPU to carry out the operation. If an arithmetic or logic operation is required, the control unit signals that the ALU is to carry it out.

Once a cycle is complete, the next one starts.

Worked example

State what is done at each stage of the fetch-decode-execute cycle. **(3 marks)**

Fetch: The next instruction to be executed is transferred from the RAM to the CPU.

Decode: The CU decodes the instruction by looking it up in the CPU's instruction set.

Execute: The CU then carries out the instruction. It instructs the ALU if calculations need to be performed.

If a question uses the command '**state**', you only need to state your answer, not explain it.

Now try this

Describe how program instructions stored in memory are processed by the central processing unit (CPU). **(3 marks)**

The need for secondary storage

Secondary storage provides long-term storage for programs and data.

Why secondary storage is needed

A computer's main memory is short-term. It only holds programs and data while they are being used by the CPU. When the power is switched off, main memory is wiped clean.

Secondary storage, on the other hand, is **non-volatile**. It does not need an uninterruptable power supply and can therefore provide long-term storage for programs and data. Without secondary storage, a program and all its associated data would have to be keyed in every time it was required.

A computer's main memory is its **primary storage**. It provides the CPU with fast, direct access to running programs and their data. A computer's hard drive provides **secondary storage** and stores programs and data when they are not in use.

How primary and secondary storage work together

- When a user opens an application, it is loaded into main memory from secondary storage.
- Any data files that are opened for use in that application are also loaded into main memory.
- When the user saves a file, it is transferred from main memory into secondary storage.
- When the application is closed, it is removed from main memory.

Differences between primary and secondary storage

Primary storage	Secondary storage
Volatile and power dependent. Its contents are lost when the power is switched off.	Non-volatile. Its content is retained even when the power is switched off.
Short-term	Long-term
It is directly accessed by the CPU.	Programs and data must be transferred to memory in order for them to be accessed by the CPU.
Limited storage capacity (between 500 MiB and 8 GiB) and only limited scope for expansion.	Large storage capacity (a magnetic hard drive can store up to 4 TiB of data). Can be expanded by using external devices, such as portable hard drives and USB memory sticks.

Worked example

Target grade 4-6

Describe **one** reason a computer needs both primary and secondary storage. **(4 marks)**

Primary storage is needed to provide the CPU with fast, direct access to the program instructions and data that it is currently using. It only retains its contents temporarily. Secondary storage is non-volatile and is needed to keep programs and data for the long term when they are not in use.

Another reason is that main memory is limited in size so it can only hold a small amount of data. There is practically no limit to the number of programs and the amount of data that can be accommodated in secondary storage.

Without secondary storage, computers would not be able to swap between tasks quickly. This would prevent them from being general purpose machines.

Now try this

Target grade 4-6

Describe how volatile storage differs from non-volatile storage. **(2 marks)**

Types of secondary storage

There are three main types of secondary storage: magnetic, optical and solid-state.

Magnetic storage

Magnetic storage devices, such as hard disk drives (HDDs) and magnetic tape drives, use magnetic storage.

An HDD contains a stack of circular, metal platters that spin at high speed. Both surfaces of each platter are coated with a substance that can be magnetised.

Each platter has its own read-write head.

To write data: an electromagnet in the read-write head magnetises the surface of the platter to one of two polarities: north-south or south-north. These represent 1 or 0 respectively. Data is stored on a series of concentric tracks, subdivided into sectors.

To read data: the read-write head detects the magnetic state of the platter.

Optical storage

Optical storage devices, such as CD and DVD drives, use patterns of light to store data on removable disks.

To write data: a laser is used to burn the surface of the disk, changing its form to become more reflective or less reflective. Reflective areas are called **lands**; less reflective areas are called **pits**. A land represents 1 and a pit 0.

Data is stored as a series of lands and pits on a single track that spirals out from the centre of the disk.

To read data: a laser beam is shone onto the surface of the disk. A pit reflects light more dimly than a land. The amount of light reflected off the surface is detected by a light sensor and translated into 1s and 0s.

Solid-state storage

Portable computing devices, such as mobile phones and smart watches, use solid-state storage. It consists of a grid of transistors.

To write data: an electrical current is applied to the transistor. This forces electrons through a barrier, trapping them in pools. A full pool represents 0 and an empty pool 1.

To read data: a small voltage is applied. If the electron pool is empty, the transistor turns on and a 1 is read out. If it is full, the transistor does not turn on and a 0 is read out.

Worked example

Target grade 4-6

Explain **two** reasons solid-state storage is the best choice for storing data on a phone.   **(4 marks)**

Solid-state storage is very robust and is unlikely to be damaged if the phone is dropped or banged, because it has no moving parts. Solid-state storage consumes very little power, so it is not too much of a drain on the phone's battery.

Comparison of different storage technologies

	Used in	Advantages	Disadvantages
Magnetic	• Internal/external hard drives • Tape drives	• High capacity • Fast data access	• Has moving parts that will eventually fail • Noisy
Optical	• CD, DVD and Blu-ray drives	• Portable • Disks are cheap	• Slow to access • Prone to scratches
Solid-state	• Solid-state drives • USB sticks • SSD cards • Mobile devices and wearables	• Very fast data access • No moving parts • Low power • Quiet	• Relatively expensive • Has a limited number of read-write cycles

Now try this

Target grade 4-6

A company backs up its business-critical data to an external magnetic hard drive every night.

Give **three** features of an external hard drive that make it suitable for this purpose.   **(3 marks)**

Embedded systems

An embedded system is a small computer on a chip, that performs a dedicated task within a bigger system. Most embedded systems work in **real-time** – they must respond immediately to an external event or request.

Features of embedded systems

- single-purpose – designed for a specific task
- customised hardware and software
- limited memory and processing power
- low power consumption
- wireless connectivity

- minimal or no user interface
- small physical size
- responsive to their environment
- low maintenance
- usually operate in real time

Hardware components of an embedded system

A long-life battery to power the system.

Sensors and other input devices to supply information from the outside world.

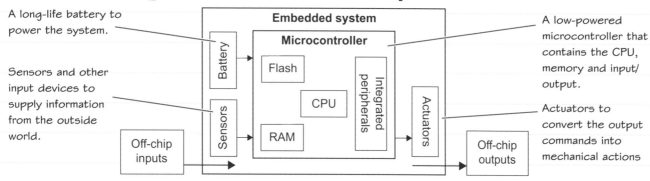

A low-powered microcontroller that contains the CPU, memory and input/output.

Actuators to convert the output commands into mechanical actions

Plus, **firmware** – the program that tells the device what to do. Once installed on the device, firmware does not need to be modified.

Examples of devices that use embedded systems

- A washing machine that regulates water usage according to the size of its load.
- A drinks dispenser that sends a reorder request to the supplier when stock is running low.
- An insulin pump that monitors blood glucose levels and delivers insulin to the patient.
- An anti-lock braking system that prevents a vehicle from skidding.
- A burglar alarm that sends a message to the homeowner's phone if it detects an intruder.

Worked example

Target grade 4-6

Describe how the embedded system in a car navigation system alerts the driver when they exceed the speed limit. **(5 marks)**

The navigation system uses satellite signals received via its GPS antenna/receiver to calculate the car's position. It uses data from on-board sensors to calculate the car's speed. It checks the speed limit of the road on which the car is travelling using a map that is stored in the system's onboard memory. It outputs a warning to the display/speaker if the car breaks the speed limit.

> If you get a question like this make sure you identify the input(s), processing, output(s) and connectivity of the system.

The internet of things (IoT)

The IoT is a network of physical objects that use embedded systems and wireless technology to collect and exchange data with little or no human interaction. There are several privacy and security issues associated with it. For example, many IoT devices are dispatched from factories with a default password set. If purchasers do not change the password, hackers can gain access to the device using a simple script.

Now try this

Target grade 4-6

A dishwasher must maintain the water it uses at the correct temperature for the programme selected. Describe how the embedded system in the dishwasher can make this happen. **(2 marks)**

Operating system 1

The operating system (OS) is the program that acts as an **interface** between the hardware and other software in a computer system, enabling them to communicate with each other. It also provides a way for users to interact with the computer. Microsoft Windows, Apple iOS and Linux are three well-known operating systems.

Main tasks performed by an operating system

- **Process management:** overseeing the execution of programs by the CPU and allocating each of them a share of main memory and CPU time.
- **File management:** organising and keeping track of the contents of secondary storage, managing files and folders and using permissions to control user access to programs and files.
- **User management:** providing a user interface to enable users to interact with the computer.
- **Peripheral management:** communicating with device drivers to control peripheral devices.

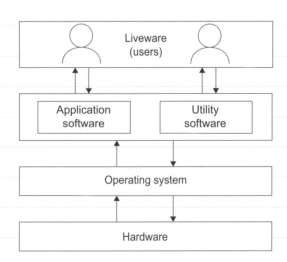

Process management

When a program is opened, it is copied from secondary storage into main memory so that it can be executed by the CPU. While they are stored in memory, programs are referred to as **processes**. Modern computers are **multitasking** – they can execute several processes concurrently (at the same time).

Since the CPU can only execute one instruction at a time, it is up to the OS to ensure that every process loaded into main memory gets a share of CPU time. The OS uses a **scheduling algorithm** to do this.

Memory management

When a process is loaded into main memory from secondary storage, the OS allocates it a block of addresses called **pages**.

Occasionally, a computer's memory may become full. When this happens, the OS frees up space by temporarily moving inactive processes out of main memory into an area of the hard drive designated as **virtual memory**. It uses a **paging algorithm** to determine which processes to swap out. Processes are swapped back in again when it is their turn to use the CPU.

Round-robin

Round-robin is a commonly used scheduling algorithm.

- Each process is allocated a time slice, with higher priority tasks being given more time slices.
- While they are waiting their turn to use the CPU, processes are held in a queue. The process at the front of the queue is next in line to use the CPU.
- During its time slice, a process has exclusive use of the CPU.
- At the end of its time slice, if the process is unfinished it goes to the back of the queue to wait for its next turn.

Worked example
Target grade 4-6

Explain **one** advantage and **one** disadvantage of the round-robin scheduling algorithm. **(4 marks)**

All processes will eventually be completed, because every process gets a turn.

Processes may have to wait a long time to complete, because there are a lot of them waiting in the queue.

Now try this
Target grade 4-6

Describe how multitasking works on a computer with a single CPU. **(3 marks)**

Operating system 2

Three important functions performed by the operating system (OS) are file, user and peripheral management.

File management

The OS is responsible for managing and keeping track of the files stored on a computer's hard drive. Files are stored in a hierarchical tree structure.

The tree elements are called 'nodes'. The lines connecting elements are called 'branches'. The top node of the tree is the root directory. A directory is a folder containing other items. Nodes lower down are either sub-directories or files.

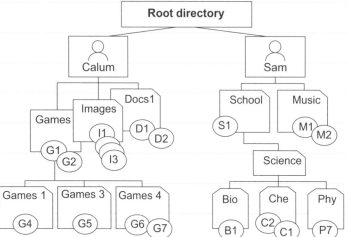

User management

Access control: In shared computers and networks, the OS uses login names and passwords and/or some form of biometric identification to authenticate users and control who can log on.

User interface: The OS provides a user interface to enable users to interact with the computer.

Graphical user interface (GUI): A GUI, such as Windows or Android, has windows, icons, drop-down menus and pointers.

Command line interface (CLI): A CLI only allows users to type in commands. They are mainly used by expert users, who want more control over the function of the computer.

File permissions control who can do what with each file.

A user can be granted one of four levels of access to files:

- **Read:** They can only view contents of files.
- **Write:** They can read and make changes to files but cannot delete them.
- **Execute:** They can run files (assuming they are executable).
- **Delete:** Gives full access rights, meaning the user can read, write and delete files.

The OS enforces the permissions associated with each user.

Peripheral management

A peripheral device is an additional item of hardware, such as a printer, a keyboard, a graphics card or a microphone that is connected to a computer.

The OS uses specialist programs called **device drivers** to enable it to communicate with peripheral devices. The drivers are installed on the computer's hard drive and have to be kept up-to-date so that peripherals continue to work as expected.

Worked example
Target grade 4-9

Describe how the operating system allocates space on the hard drive to a file. **(5 marks)**

Files are broken up into blocks of a fixed size. Each block is placed in an empty space on the disk. Blocks may not be contiguous (next to each other). Any left-over space where a block is not complete is known as 'slack space'. The OS keeps track of the starting point of each block and its sequence number for files larger than one block.

Now try this
Target grade 4-6

1 Describe how the operating system organises files on a hard drive. **(3 marks)**

2 Describe how the operating system retrieves a file from secondary storage. **(4 marks)**

Utility software

Utility software is a collection of small, specialised programs, each of which performs a specific task.

Data compression software

Purpose: To reduce the size of a file so that it takes up less space in secondary storage and is quicker to transfer across networks.

How it works: It repackages (lossless compression) or removes (lossy compression) some of a file's data to reduce its size.

File repair software

Purpose: To recover data from and repair files that have become corrupted by a computer malfunction or cyberattack.

How it works: It scans the damaged file, extracts as much data from it as possible and stores it in a new usable file.

Disk defragmentation software

Purpose: To speed up access to files stored on a magnetic hard drive.

How it works: It rearranges individual file blocks for each file so that they are stored in contiguous (adjoining) blocks on the disk.

Backup software

Purpose: To keep a copy of files so that, should a file get lost or damaged, the most recent backup can be restored.

How it works: Backup copies of files are made at regular intervals and stored on a separate device in a different location to the live working environment – possibly in the cloud.

> Solid-state drives get just as fragmented as magnetic hard drives but, because they have no moving parts, it does not affect the data access speed.

Why fragmentation occurs

When a file is saved to the hard drive, it gets split up into blocks. Ideally, all blocks belonging to one file are saved in adjoining sectors on the disk. As files are changed, blocks have to be saved wherever there is a free space.

Fragmentation slows down read operations, because more disk accesses are needed to retrieve all the blocks of a single file.

Anti-malware software

Purpose: To protect computer systems and data from damage caused by malware, such as viruses, worms and spyware.

How it works: Some types of anti-malware software use a database of malware signatures (the patterns associated with a known piece of malware). If the anti-malware detects a file that has a pattern that matches a known signature, it deletes or quarantines it.

Some use **heuristic analysis** to detect suspicious behaviour, such as a program that tries to remain resident in memory after it has finished executing.

Worked example

Target grade **4-6**

Calum installs an update for the anti-malware software on his laptop.

1 Explain **one** reason it is important to keep anti-malware software up-to-date.

(2 marks)

Anti-malware software needs to be updated to include signatures of new viruses in its database, enabling it to detect them. This is vital as new viruses are constantly being written and released.

2 Give **one** reason why an anti-malware program that uses a malware signature database may not identify all malware.

(1 mark)

The signatures of very new malware may not be in its database.

Now try this

Target grade **4-6**

Manjit has made a recording of her school play. She plans to upload it to her social media account for her friends to view.

Explain what type of utility software Manjit should use before she uploads the file. Explain why. **(2 marks)**

Robust software

A program is deemed robust if it can handle unexpected actions without crashing or producing incorrect output and if it is free from vulnerabilities that could be exploited by criminals.

Code vulnerabilities

A program may have hidden weaknesses that could pose a security threat. Criminals can exploit such code vulnerabilities to cause damage or gain access to sensitive information.

Known vulnerabilities

Some programming languages contain known vulnerabilities.

For example, programs written in C can access computer memory directly. This allows hackers to implement a 'backdoor' entry into systems.

Three things programmers can do to make their programs robust:

- ☑ adhere to good programming practices
- ☑ carry out regular code reviews
- ☑ keep an audit trail.

Bad programming practices include:
- ☒ poor planning that does not take account of potential security issues
- ☒ using a quick fix rather than taking time to solve a problem properly
- ☒ poorly structured code that does not adhere to agreed standards
- ☒ insufficient testing.

Code reviews

The purpose of a code review is:

- to check that software adheres to agreed standards
- to find any instances of inefficient code
- to identify potential vulnerabilities.

Reviews are carried out by other programmers or by specialised software that checks the code to make sure it meets a pre-defined set of rules. It can detect bugs and security issues and may suggest ways to fix them.

If a code review identifies any issues, they must be put right before proceeding any further.

Audit trails

An audit trail helps improve accountability by keeping track of who made what changes and when during the development process. Should a problem be discovered, it can be tracked back to its source and the code **rolled back** to a version before the flaw was introduced.

Version control software is often used alongside audit trails, especially when a team of programmers is working on a large or complex project. It uses a database to keep track of every modification to the code. If a mistake is made, programmers can revert to an earlier version.

Worked example

Aisha is conducting a code review. One thing she must do is check for programming language-specific vulnerabilities.

1 Give **four** other things she must look out for. **(4 marks)**

2 Define what is meant by a 'language-specific vulnerability'. **(2 marks)**

1
- Errors in the code.
- Code inefficiencies.
- Bad programming practices.
- Requirements are fully implemented.

Other correct answers would be:
- If the code conforms to agreed style guidelines.
- Security vulnerabilities.

2 A known weakness in the way in which a high-level language performs a particular operation, which can be exploited by hackers.

Now try this

Explain **one** reason why a 'quick fix' solution to a code problem may introduce vulnerabilities. **(2 marks)**

Programming languages

A programming language consists of a set of instructions and syntax rules, which are used to write code. Programming languages can be grouped into two categories, low-level and high-level, based on how close they are to a recognisable 'human' language.

Low-level languages

Machine code and **assembly language** are low-level languages that work directly with a computer's hardware. A programmer must have detailed knowledge of a computer's architecture in order to write a program in a low-level language. They must be familiar with the CPU's instruction set (binary instructions, **opcodes**, that it recognises and acts upon).

Machine code is written in binary, with even a simple program made up of thousands of 1s and 0s. This makes it extremely difficult for programmers to write and debug.

Assembly language is a bit easier for humans to work with. Instead of binary, it uses short memorable keywords called **mnemonics** to represent instructions. Programs have to be translated into machine code before they can be executed by the CPU.

Use: Device drivers and firmware for embedded systems are often written in low-level languages.

High-level languages

High-level languages, such as Java and Python, are closer to human languages than low-level languages. They use keywords such as 'print', 'if' and 'return'.

High-level languages are **problem-oriented**. They enable programmers to focus on their program's logic, rather than on how it will be implemented on a computer's hardware.

High-level languages come with libraries of ready-made functions, integrated development environments and editing tools to make it easier to write code.

A program written in a high-level language must be translated before it can be executed by a CPU.

A single line of code written in a high-level language often requires multiple lines of machine-code instructions to implement.

Use: Most software is now developed using a high-level language.

Low-level languages	High-level languages
⊗ Are difficult and time-consuming to use.	✓ Are programmer-friendly.
⊗ Have few tools to help with maintenance and debugging.	✓ Have tools that make maintenance and debugging easier.
⊗ Are machine-specific – programs written in a low-level language will not run on a computer with a different type of CPU.	✓ Are machine-independent (portable) – they will run on computers with different types of CPU.
✓ Interact directly with the hardware, enabling memory to be used efficiently.	⊗ Are generally less memory efficient.

Worked example

A program written in a high-level language will run on computers with different types of CPU, whereas one written in a low-level language is machine-specific. Explain this difference. **(3 marks)**

Programs written in a high-level language focus on the program logic and do not concern themselves with how it will be implemented on a particular computer architecture. Programs written in a low-level language use the instruction set of a specific CPU.

Now try this

A program is needed to control an embedded system with very limited on-chip memory.

Explain **one** reason why a programmer may decide to write the program in a low-level language. **(2 marks)**

Interpreters and compilers

Programs written in a high-level language must be translated into machine code before the processor can execute them. Compilers, interpreters and assemblers are examples of translators.

Compiler

A **compiler** translates the source code into a stand-alone machine code program (object code) that can then be executed by the processor.

- ✓ The translation is done once only and as a separate process.
- ✓ The program that is run is already translated into machine code so it can be executed more rapidly.
- ✓ It protects the software from competitors who would otherwise be able to see the source code.
- ✗ If it encounters any errors, it carries on trying to compile the program and reports the errors at the end. The programmers then have to use the error messages to identify and remove the bugs.
- ✗ You cannot change the program without going back to the original source code, editing that and recompiling.

Interpreter

An **interpreter** translates the high-level code line by line into machine code. It is needed each time the program is run.

- ✓ When an error is found, the interpreter reports it, stops and pinpoints the error so that the programmer knows where it has occurred.
- ✓ The code is not platform-specific and can be run on different operating systems and platforms as long as there is an interpreter.
- ✓ The program can be easily edited as it always exists as source code.
- ✗ Every line has to be translated each time it is executed, and therefore it is slower to run.

Assemblers

Assemblers translate the **mnemonics of assembly language** into machine-code instructions. Assembly language is very similar to machine code. There is one assembly language instruction for each machine-code instruction.

Worked example

1 Explain one reason why program code developed using a high-level language must be translated.

(4 marks)

Instructions must be translated into machine code, because that is the only language that the processor can execute.

2 A compiler or an interpreter can be used to translate the code. State **one** advantage and **one** disadvantage of using each of these translators.

(2 marks)

An advantage of using an interpreter is that it will stop when it finds an error and pinpoint the error for the developer, but a disadvantage is that it is slower to execute the program because each line must be translated each time it is run. An advantage of using a compiler is that the translation needs to be done only once, but a disadvantage is that if the program needs to be changed, then the original source code has to be edited and recompiled.

Now try this

1 Jaxon wants to write a games app for a mobile phone. Give **one** reason why it would be better for Jaxon to use a compiled rather than an interpreted language for this purpose. **(1 mark)**

2 Esme has an idea for a self-watering plant pot device. Give one reason why it would be better for Esme to use an interpreted rather than a compiled language for this purpose. **(1 mark)**

Networks

A network is an arrangement of two or more computing devices connected together in order to communicate with each other and share resources. One way of differentiating networks is by the size of the area they cover. A **LAN** covers a relatively small area, whereas a **WAN** covers a large geographical area and connects multiple LANs together.

Reasons for connecting computers on a network

- ✅ To share data and software.
- ✅ To share printers, hard drives and other hardware peripherals.
- ✅ To share internet connections and services, such as the web and web-based software.
- ✅ To provide centralised support and backup services.

- ✅ To enable the rapid deployment of new software and updates.
- ✅ To enable people to communicate with each other using services such as email and video conferencing.
- ✅ To support collaborative working.

Local area network (LAN)

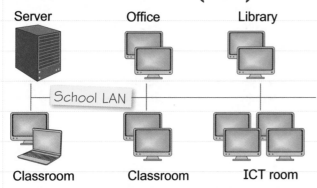

A **local area network** is a network in a small area such as a home, school, office building or group of buildings on a single site. It exists within a small geographical area. A LAN is usually managed by a local manager or team at the site. Many people have a home LAN that allows the members of the household to access the internet using a wireless router.

The internet is a global system of interconnected computer networks. Hyperlinks can take you from a host computer in one LAN to a computer in another. The internet is therefore an example of a huge WAN.

Wide area network (WAN)

Wide area networks connect separate LANs over a large geographical area to form a network of networks. Large companies can connect LANs at their different sites in order to share resources and data. Computers in a WAN can communicate with computers and users in other locations.

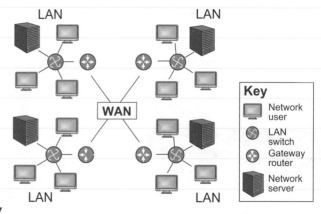

Key
- 🖥 Network user
- LAN switch
- Gateway router
- Network server

The WAN will be managed by several different people or parts of an organisation working together (collective ownership). Alternatively, each LAN could be managed independently (distributed ownership).

Worked example
Target grade 1-3

Ivy is a graphic designer. She stores her designs on a network-attached storage (NAS) drive and uses a file transfer service to send designs. Ivy uses different types of networks for different tasks.

1 Name the type of network she uses to store designs on the NAS drive. **(1 mark)**
2 Name the type of network she uses to send designs to clients. **(1 mark)**

1 LAN, 2 WAN

Now try this
Target grade 4-6

A retailer wants to share data between its head office and 200 high-street stores.

1 Describe **one** reason the business would use a WAN rather than a LAN for this purpose.
(2 marks)

2 The business has a central IT team, based at head office. Describe **one** way an IT technician could use the WAN to investigate a fault with a network-connected device in one of the stores.
(2 marks)

The internet

The internet is a global system of interconnected networks. It links together billions of digital devices worldwide. It is the world's largest public WAN.

A network of networks

No single organisation owns the internet. It is a network of networks – some privately owned, some public. It is connected via super-fast fibre-optic cables and satellites, which together form the **backbone of the internet**.

IP addressing

Every internet-connected device is assigned a unique IP address so that it can send and receive data. IP stands for **internet protocol**.

 Links See pages 52 and 53 for more information about protocols.

There are two versions of IP – **IPv4** and **IPv6**. IPv4 dates back to the 1970s and uses 32-bit addresses – sufficient for 4 billion devices to be uniquely identified. This is no longer enough. IPv6 is needed to make more addresses available. It uses 128-bit addresses, enough to generate 340 trillion trillion unique IDs.

Most devices use a **dynamic IP address**. This is allocated to them from a communal pool when they connect to the internet and returned when they disconnect. Next time they connect, their IP address will probably be different.

A device, such as a **router** or a **web server**, is permanently connected to the internet with a static IP address that never changes.

A **domain name** is a human-friendly form of an IP address. Domain names, such as www.pearson.com, are much easier to use than their equivalent IP addresses.

Worked example

Target grade 1-3

1 Explain the role of IP addresses in internet communications. **(2 marks)**

2 Both IPv4 and IPv6 addresses are used to identify devices on the internet. Explain **one** reason why IPv6 has been introduced. **(3 marks)**

1 IP addresses are used to uniquely identify every device connected to the internet, so that they can send and receive data.

2 The supply of IPv4 addresses is running out because the number of internet-connected devices has grown much faster than expected. IPv6 uses 128 bits so it can generate many more unique addresses.

URL

URL stands for **uniform resource locator**. It is the complete web address of a particular web page, image or other resource on the internet.

What happens when a web page is requested

When a user types a URL into their browser's address bar, the browser sends the URL to a **DNS** server, asking for its corresponding IP address.

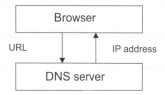

DNS is short for **domain name system**. Its purpose is to match domain names to IP addresses.

Once it receives the IP address from the DNS server, the browser sends an HTTP page request to the **web server** that holds the page data.

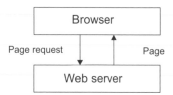

The server finds the correct files and sends them to the browser. Once it receives the data, the browser renders the page and displays it on the screen.

Now try this

Target grade 4-6

Smarts Leisure Group has a company website that customers can use to book holidays.

Explain **one** reason why the web server that hosts the Smarts Leisure website should have a static IP address. **(3 marks)**

Packet switching

Data travels across the internet in packets using a method called packet switching.

Packet switching

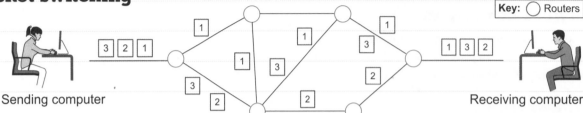

Key: ◯ Routers

Sending computer

Receiving computer

❶ The sender's large file is broken up into smaller packets.

❷ Packets are directed to their destination by routers. Routers inspect the packets and decide the most efficient path to the next router.

❸ Packets take different routes across the network. They may not arrive in the correct order. A packet will need to be forwarded between several routers before it reaches its destination.

❹ The receiving computer reassembles them in the correct order using information in the packet headers.

 Links See page 53 for details of the TCP/IP protocol stack that defines the rules governing the transmission of data over the internet.

Routers

Routers form a physical connection between two or more networks and forward data packets from one network to another.

Routing table

When a router receives an incoming packet, it:

- finds the packet's destination address
- uses its **routing table** to select the most efficient route for the packet to take on the next leg of its journey.

Routers keep each other informed of traffic conditions on their part of the internet.
If a route is congested, the router will send packets a different way.
Data packets from the same transmission may travel to their destination via different routes and may therefore arrive out of sequence.

Data packets

A data packet consists of a **payload**, a **header** and a **footer**.

Header	IP address of destination IP address of source Sequence number Total number of packets Checksum
Payload	Part of the data for a web page, an email, a streamed movie, etc.
Footer	End of packet flag

On arrival at the destination, the receiving computer:

- checks that each of the packets is complete and uncorrupted
- checks that all the data packets that were sent have been received
- if necessary, asks the source computer to resend a corrupt or missing packet
- reassembles the packets in the correct order.

Worked example

Target grade 1-3

State **one** benefit of a packet switching network. **(1 mark)**

If there is a problem or congestion in one part of the network, then the packets can be sent by a different route to avoid it.

Now try this

Target grade 4-6

Madison sends an email to her friend Eliza. The email is split up into packets for transmission across the internet. A header is attached to each packet. Two items included in a packet header are a sequence number and a checksum.

Explain **one** reason why these items are needed.

(4 marks)

Wired versus wireless

Wired and wireless **transmission media** (communication channels) carry data between devices on a network.

Wired

Devices can be physically connected to each other using a **cable**. The most common cable material is **copper wire**. Made of thin strands of copper, it transmits data as electrical pulses. **Fibre-optic cable** is the modern alternative. It is made from very thin strands of glass that transmit data as pulses of light. Fibre-optic cable offers advantages over copper, but it is considerably more expensive and – because it is made out of glass – more fragile and difficult to handle.

	Copper wire	Fibre-optic cable
Range	Up to 100 m	Up to 80 km
Bandwidth	Up to 10 Gbps	Up to 100 Gbps
Latency	Susceptible to electrical interference	Immune to electrical interference
Usage	Used to connect devices on a LAN	Used for long distance data traffic

Range is the distance over which data can be transferred.
Bandwidth is the volume of data that can be transferred. It is measured in bits per second (bps).
Latency is the time lag between data leaving its source and arriving at its destination. It is measured in milliseconds. Electrical interference is one factor that affects latency.

Wireless

Wireless transmission media use **radio** waves to transmit data through the air. **Wi-Fi** is the most well-known wireless transmission medium and has been around the longest, but there are several other alternatives that have different ranges and power requirements.

	Range	Power consumption	Uses
Wi-Fi	Up to 100 m, but physical objects can obstruct the signal	High	To network devices in LANs and to connect devices to the internet.
Bluetooth	Up to 10 m	Low	To pair devices over short distances, e.g. linking a headset to a phone.
Zigbee	Up to 100 m	Low	Home automation and Internet of Things, e.g. smart light bulbs.
RFID	Up to 1 m	Low	Security tags, passports and implants.
NFC	Close proximity – around 10 cm	Very low or none	Contactless payment systems.

Worked example

Target grade 7-9

The UK issues RFID-embedded passports. The RFID chip contains biometric information used to authenticate the identity of the passport holder.

Explain **two** reasons why RFID is suitable for this purpose.   **(4 marks)**

There is no need for a physical cable connection, because data is transmitted wirelessly between the RFID chip and reader. The risk of the data transmission being intercepted by a third party is reduced because the chip and reader must be within 1 m of each other to transfer data.

You could also say that an RFID is suitable for embedding within physical objects because the chip does not need its own power supply.

Now try this

Target grade 4-6

Give **three** reasons why fibre-optic cable is better suited than copper wire to provide high-speed broadband connectivity.   **(3 marks)**

Connectivity on a LAN

Devices on a LAN may be connected using wired or wireless transmission media (communication channels). Some networks are formed using a combination of both.

Wired versus wireless LANs

There are advantages and disadvantages associated with using both wired and wireless transmission media to create a LAN.

	Wired	Wireless
Installation	Difficult. Every network device needs its own dedicated cable.	Easy. A wireless LAN (WLAN) does not take long to install, and adding a new device is easy. Only the wireless access points (WAPs) need to be connected by cable.
Flexibility	Limited. The number and location of cable connections is fixed. Making changes once the LAN is up and running is likely to be disruptive and time-consuming.	Easy. Devices can be moved around without losing the connection, providing they do not go out of signal range. New users can easily be added – they just need to be given the network ID (SSID) and a password.
Range	Long. Up to 100 m. Range may be further enhanced if a signal booster is installed.	Shorter. Walls and other physical obstacles may obstruct the signal.
Bandwidth	High. Up to 10 Gigabits per second (Gbps) per connection.	Low. Up to 3.2 Gbps. All the active devices on the network must share the available bandwidth.
Latency	Low. The cables have layers of protective coverings making them less susceptible to interference.	High. Susceptible to interference from other wireless networks or devices.
Security	Good. It is impossible to tap into physical cables without being in the same location as the cable.	Poor. Anyone within range can intercept transmissions.

Many networks use a combination of wired and wireless transmission media.

In a **mixed network**, some devices, such as printers and whiteboards, are directly connected via cables, while others, such as laptops, games consoles and phones, connect wirelessly. The router assigns an internal IP address to each device irrespective of its method of connection. This enables them all to become part of the same network.

> Another reason for connecting the TV to the router by cable is to ensure that it has enough bandwidth to stream content from the internet.

Worked example

Target grade 7-9

Some devices on a home network, including a TV and a NAS drive are connected to the network by cables. Others connect to the network wirelessly. Describe **one** benefit of this network setup. **(2 marks)**

Devices that have a fixed location within the house may as well be cabled in, freeing up the available wireless bandwidth for devices that do not have a fixed location to use.

Now try this

Target grade 7-9

A school is considering whether to install a cable or wireless network. Discuss the benefits and drawbacks of each type of network when they are used in a school situation. **(6 marks)**

Network speeds

The speed of a network is its **data transfer rate** – the number of bits that can be transferred from one device to another across the network in a specified period of time. Data transfer rate is measured in bits per second. As modern technology is capable of transferring large volumes of data at high speeds, data transfer rates are usually given in megabits per second (Mbps).

Units of measurement

Data transfer rate (speed) is measured in base-10 units.

Unit	Abbrev.	No. of bits
bits per second	bps	1
bytes per second	Bps	8
kilobits per second	Kbps	1000
megabits per second	Mbps	1000^2
gigabits per second	Gbps	1000^3

File size is measured in base-2 units.

Unit	Abbrev.	No. of bits
bit		1
byte		8
kibibyte	KiB	1024×8
mebibyte	MiB	$1024^2 \times 8$
gibibyte	GiB	$1024^3 \times 8$
tebibyte	TiB	$1024^4 \times 8$

Formula

The formula to calculate the length of time it takes for a file to reach its destination is:

Time (in seconds) = File size (in bits) ÷ Data transfer rate (in bps)

Given any two of the variables, you can rearrange the formula to find the missing one:

File size (in bits) = Time (in seconds) × Data transfer rate (in bps)

Data transfer rate (in bps) = File size (in bits) ÷ Time (in seconds)

Worked example

Target grade 4-6

1 A 55 MiB file is transmitted across a network.

Construct an expression to calculate how many seconds it will take to transmit the file at a transmission rate of 38 Mbps. You do not need to do the calculation. **(5 marks)**

> 'Transmission rate' means the same as 'speed' or 'data transfer rate'.

$$\frac{55 \times 1024 \times 1024 \times 8}{38 \times 1000 \times 1000}$$

← Convert the file size into bits.
← Divide the file size by the data transfer rate.
← Convert the data transfer rate into bits per second.

2 A 15 GiB file takes 18 seconds to download.

Construct an expression to calculate the speed of the network in megabits per second. You do not need to do the calculation. **(3 marks)**

> Speed = file size in bits ÷ time in seconds.

$$\frac{15 \times 1024 \times 1024 \times 1024 \times 8}{18 \times 1000 \times 1000}$$

← The speed must be given in Mbps.

> In both questions, you are asked to construct an expression, but not to actually do the calculation.

Now try this

Target grade 4-6

A network transfers data at 3.2 Gbps.

Construct an expression to show how many bytes can be transmitted in 15 seconds. You do not need to do the calculation. **(3 marks)**

Network protocols

Protocols define the rules that govern how data must be formatted, transmitted and received on a network. Without protocols, network devices, such as hubs, servers, routers, switches, laptops and phones, would not be able to understand the electronic signals that they send to each other.

Protocols

Protocols are needed to ensure that data is sent and received accurately, and that it is sent to the correct address on a network. Protocols need to include:

- data formats, to ensure that data can be exchanged consistently and correctly
- address formats, to identify senders and recipients and to ensure that data goes to the right places
- routing, to provide the right information so that data can flow through networks correctly.

Protocol layers

Network protocols work in layers. Those in the top layer are the ones that users see; those at the bottom handle the technicalities of converting data from binary into electrical, light or radio signals so that they can be transmitted across a network.

TCP/IP is a collection of protocols, known as a stack, that determines how data is transmitted over the internet. It has four layers. The top level is the application layer. Applications such as file transfer, web browsers and email operate at this level.

Links TCP/IP see page 53.

Application layer protocols

FTP	**File Transfer Protocol** provides the rules for file transfer between computers. It is often used to transfer files that are too large for attachment to emails.
HTTP	**Hypertext Transfer Protocol** provides the rules to be followed by a web browser and a web server when requesting and supplying information. It is used for sending requests from a web client (a browser) to a web server and returning web content from the server back to the client.
HTTPS	**Secure HTTP** ensures that communications between a host and client are secure by encrypting communications.
SMTP	**Simple Mail Transfer Protocol** provides the rules for sending email messages from client to server and then from server to server until it reaches its destination.
POP	**Post Office Protocol** is used by a client to retrieve emails from a mail server. All of the emails are downloaded when there is a connection between client and server. Messages are deleted from the email server once they have been downloaded.
IMAP	**Internet Message Access Protocol.** Unlike POP, the messages do not have to be downloaded. They can be read and stored on the message server. This is better for users with many different devices as they can be read from all devices rather than being downloaded to just one.

Worked example

Target grade 4-6

Amin wants to visit a specific web page. He types its URL into the address bar of his browser.

Describe the role of the hypertext transfer protocol (HTTP) in retrieving the web page and getting it to Amin's browser. **(3 marks)**

The browser and the server use HTTP commands to communicate with each other. The browser sends an HTTP GET request to the web server requesting the web page. The web server sends back an HTTP response containing the requested web page.

Now try this

Target grade 4-6

Describe one difference between the POP and IMAP email protocols. **(2 marks)**

The TCP/IP model

TCP/IP is a hierarchical set (or stack) of network protocols, that work together to enable devices to communicate with each other over the internet. Each layer in the stack is responsible for a different aspect of communication.

The four-layer protocol stack

Outgoing data is passed from the sending computer down the stack from one layer to the next until it gets to the bottom. It is then transmitted over the internet by the protocols in the link layer.

On arrival at the receiving end, incoming data is passed up the stack to the receiving computer.

Individual layers of the stack do not know how the layers above and below them function. They only know how to pass data to them.

Each layer may contain several protocols, each providing a service suitable to the function of that layer. For example, a file transfer protocol and an email protocol both provide user services, and both are part of the application layer.

Each protocol has a role to play at both the sending and receiving end.

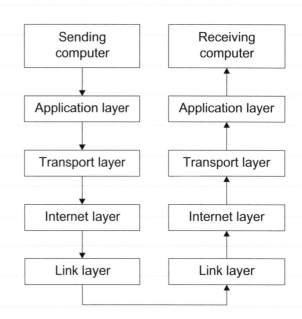

Layer	Purpose	Protocols
Application layer	**Sending:** provides the interfaces and protocols needed by the user. **Receiving:** displays received information to the user.	FTP, HTTP, HTTPS, SMTP, POP, IMAP
Transport layer	**Sending:** splits outgoing data into packets and numbers them. Adds a header containing a sequence number and a checksum to each packet. **Receiving:** checks incoming packets and sends a resend request for any that have been damaged or lost in transit. Notifies the sender when all the packets have arrived. Reassembles packets into the correct order and passes the data up to the appropriate protocol in the application layer.	TCP
Internet layer (Network layer)	**Sending:** adds the source and destination IP addresses to packet headers, enabling routers to guide each packet to its destination. **Receiving:** strips address information from incoming packet headers.	IP
Link layer (Network interface layer)	**Sending:** uses network-specific protocols to convert binary data into electrical, light or radio signals for network transmission. **Receiving side:** converts incoming signals into binary data.	Ethernet, Wi-Fi

Worked example

Target grade 4-6

Describe the role of TCP in handling incoming data packets. **(4 marks)**

TCP identifies and requests the retransmission of any lost or corrupted packets, reassembles packets in the correct order and passes the data on to the appropriate protocol in the application layer.

Now try this

Target grade 4-6

Describe the role of the link layer in sending outgoing data packets from a network-connected device to the network router. **(2 marks)**

Network topologies

The topology of a network describes how devices are physically arranged and connected together. There are three topologies that are commonly used – bus, star and mesh.

Star topology

In a star network, each computer or client is connected **individually** to a central point or **node**, which can be a hub or switch.

Star network topology

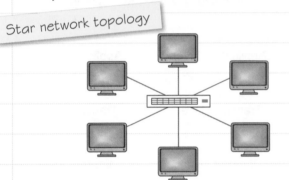

Mesh topology

In a mesh network, each computer or client is connected to at least **one other computer**.

Mesh network topology

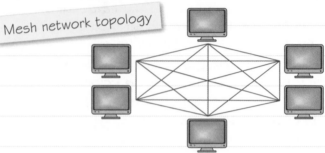

As well as sending its own signals, each computer also relays data from the others.

Using a star network

- ✓ Data is only sent to the intended computer directly.
- ✓ Network traffic is kept to a minimum.
- ✓ If one link fails, all the other devices will continue to operate.
- ✓ It is easy to add new devices without disrupting the network.
- ✗ If the central point fails, then so will the entire network.
- ✗ Requires a lot of cable because each computer connects individually to a central component.

Using a mesh network

- ✓ Commonly connected on wireless networks where there is high demand.
- ✓ Data can be transmitted from different devices simultaneously.
- ✓ If one component fails, there is always an alternative route for data.
- ✓ Can handle high volumes of data traffic.
- ✓ Adding more devices will not slow data transmission.
- ✗ Overall cost is high. More cable is required unless a wireless network is used.
- ✗ Difficult to manage and requires expert supervision.

Bus topology

Each node (workstation or device) is connected to a main cable called a **bus**.

Bus network

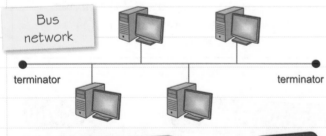

terminator   terminator

Using a bus network

- ✓ Easy to set up.
- ✓ Relatively cheap to install because only one cable is needed.
- ✓ Easy to add extra devices.
- ✗ Lots of data collisions occur when multiple devices transmit data at the same time. The devices detect collisions and resend the data, slowing down the network.
- ✗ If the main cable fails or gets damaged, the whole network will fail.
- ✗ The whole network will fail if a terminator is removed.

Worked example

Target grade **4-6**

Describe how a star topology is implemented on a wireless LAN. **(1 mark)**

The wireless router acts as central hub, with individual devices communicating directly with it.

Now try this

Target grade **4-6**

Explain **one** advantage of a mesh network over a star network. **(2 marks)**

Network security

The goal of network security is to protect a network and its data from internal and external threats.

Reasons for network security

- Ensures that only authorised users can access the network and its resources.
- Ensures that users can only access data relevant to them.
- Prevents misuse: deleting information, installing software, copying and removing data.
- Prevents damage to hardware.

> Organisations must also ensure that data stored in the cloud is secure, as cloud data centres are magnets for hackers. Sensitive or confidential data is best stored locally.

Importance of network security

- **Business success** – data on the network is vital for running an organisation. The business may fail if the data is compromised.
- **Privacy** – data stored on the network may be sensitive, e.g. medical records, and must be stored securely to comply with the law.
- **Financial** – the data may be financially valuable, e.g. details of new products and marketing campaigns.

Network vulnerabilities

An organisation's network is vulnerable to threats posed by:

- **Hackers** – those who exploit security vulnerabilities in order to gain unauthorised access to a network.
- **Insiders** – people who work for the organisation and have **authorised** access to the network. Not all insider threats are malicious. Most are caused by human error or irresponsible behaviour.
- Malicious software (**malware**), such as viruses, spyware and ransomware – designed to cause damage and disruption.

 Links You can read more about threats to digital systems on pages 64 to 66.

Penetration testing

Penetration testing is used to test a computer system or network in order to find vulnerabilities that an attacker could exploit.

- Testers take the role of hackers and try to gain unauthorised access.
- Testing also assesses the security awareness of users and demonstrates the effectiveness of network security policies.

A variety of techniques can be used.

In **black-box penetration testing** the tester is given no information about the network and must try to breach its security using the methods and techniques of a real hacker.

In **white-box penetration testing** the tester is given access to relevant network and system information. They use this to identify potential security loopholes that could be exploited by people within the organisation and outsiders.

Ethical hacking

An ethical hacker is a computer and networking expert who systematically attempts to penetrate a computer system or network on behalf of its owners for the purpose of finding security vulnerabilities that a malicious hacker could potentially exploit.

Ethical hackers are often referred to as **white-hat hackers**, to differentiate them from criminals, who are known as **black-hat hackers**.

Worked example   Target grade 4-6

Explain **one** reason why a person attempting to gain unauthorised access to a networked computer can sometimes benefit the owner of the network.   **(2 marks)**

The person may be an ethical hacker who will notify the owner of the network of any security breaches they find.

Now try this   Target grade 4-6

A company is concerned that its business-critical data could be targeted by criminals. Describe **one** way that penetration testing can help prevent this happening.   **(2 marks)**

55

Protecting networks

Organisations protect their networks by controlling who can access them and by limiting what those with access are permitted to do.

Access control

Access control limits who can log into a network and what they are permitted to do. **Authentication** is the process of determining whether a person attempting to gain access is who they claim to be.

Many organisations use some form of **multi-factor authentication** for extra security. In addition to having a valid ID and password, users must have a swipe card and/or supply some unique **biometric** information about themselves. This might be a fingerprint or the shape of their face.

Permissions enable access to files to be controlled. For example:

- Some users may not be able to view certain folders and files.
- Users can be given 'read-only' access so that they can read the files, or 'read and write' access so they can also modify them.
- At a higher level, users can be given the right to delete files and also to set other users' rights to particular files.

Physical security

The first line of defence is to **prevent unauthorised people** from entering buildings where network equipment is located.

- **Access doors** should be kept locked, and should be fitted with security recognition measures, e.g. keypads.
- **Biometric security recognition** can be used on mobile devices to authenticate users.
- **Swipe cards** containing users' details can be used for entry to a building.
- **Closed-circuit television** can be used to monitor the building's exterior and interior.
- **RFID** chips can be fitted to all equipment so that an alarm will sound if the equipment is removed.

Principle of least privilege

Network managers often apply the **principle of least privilege** when assigning file permissions. They only give users the level of access to files and software that they need to do their job.

Firewalls

- A firewall protects a network connected to a WAN such as the internet.
- It can be provided by hardware or software.
- Firewalls can be configured to prevent communications from entering the network and also programs and users from accessing the internet from within the network.

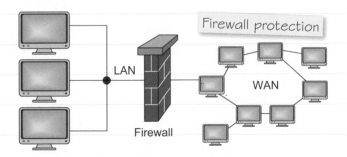

Firewall protection

LAN

WAN

Firewall

Individual computers are likely to have a software firewall installed with some default rules. A business is likely to have a hardware-based firewall, because this has greater flexibility in terms of the rules that can be applied, and can allow faster throughput of data. They are PC-like appliances that can be configured to block unwanted network traffic.

Worked example
Target grade 4-6

Give **two** reasons why the use of biometric authentication is gaining in popularity. **(2 marks)**

1 Convenience. A person's biometric characteristics are always with them and cannot be lost, stolen or forgotten.

2 Uniqueness. The algorithm used to generate a unique identifier for an individual's biometric characteristic will not generate the same identifier for a different person.

Now try this
Target grade 4-9

Describe how a firewall helps protect an organisation's network from hacking. **(4 marks)**

Environmental issues 1

The manufacture, use and disposal of digital devices has a significant impact on the environment.

Manufacture

- Large quantities of raw materials are used to make digital devices. Many, including copper and palladium, are non-renewable. Some, such as arsenic, are highly toxic.
- Mining for raw materials scars the landscape with waste and damages wildlife habitats.
- Much of the energy used in the manufacturing process comes from non-renewable fossil fuels. Burning fossil fuels contributes to global warming.
- Polluted waste water is a by-product of the manufacturing process.

Disposal

Many discarded digital devices end up as **e-waste**. Approximately 50 million tons of are produced each year. Only around 20% of e-waste is recycled.

> Illegal tipping of e-waste causes significant harm to the environment and puts lives at risk.

- E-waste may be illegally dumped in landfill sites where toxic waste substances (lead, mercury and cobalt) can get into the land and water. Severe health issues are caused by living near, or trying to salvage saleable items from e-waste dumps.
- Many computer components cannot be recycled or reused.
- Millions of tonnes of e-waste are dumped in developing countries every year.

> The Waste Electrical and Electronic Equipment (WEEE) regulations set targets for the collection, recycling and recovery of computing technology and other electronic items.

Energy consumption

Vast amounts of energy are consumed in the:

- production of computer equipment
- functioning of equipment
- online data storage in data centres
- recycling of equipment.

However, smarter technologies help to protect the environment, e.g. light sensors that turn off lights when they are not needed and route planners that reduce fuel consumption.

Energy use and digital devices

Manufacture and disposal = 70% (approx.)
- mining raw materials
- manufacturing
- packaging
- transportation
- recycling.

Use = 30% (approx.)
- powering the devices
- running global telecommunications networks
- storing vast amounts of data.

Responsible recycling

Responsible recycling can address some of the problems associated with e-waste. It can:

- reduce the potential for chemical leakage/ fires in landfills
- enable the recovery of valuable metals
- reduce the need for mining
- enable the recycling of plastic cases – these would otherwise decompose into toxic particles
- reduce the amount of harmful toxins released into the air.

Worked example

Target grade 1-3

Describe what manufacturers of digital devices must do to comply with WEEE Regulations.

(2 marks)

Manufacturers must operate a recycling program to recover recyclable materials and dispose of dangerous substances safely.

Now try this

Target grade 1-3

Data centres use around 200 terawatt hours (TWh) of electricity each year.

State **two** reasons data centres need such vast amounts of energy.   **(2 marks)**

Environmental issues 2

If digital devices are manufactured and used in a responsible way, the damaging effect they can have on the environment is reduced. Digital technology can also help to create a more sustainable world.

Short replacement cycle

The average user trades in a mobile phone for a newer model roughly once every three years. The same is true for other personal digital devices, such as tablets, smart watches and laptops. The desire to own the latest high-tech model is the main reason for upgrading.

Even when a user would prefer to keep their current device rather than replace it with a new one, manufacturers make it difficult for them to do so by:

- ⊗ using embedded batteries that are difficult to replace
- ⊗ gluing and soldering components to make repair difficult
- ⊗ inflating the price of spare parts, to make repairs expensive
- ⊗ only providing software updates and security patches for a limited time.

Consequences of the short replacement cycle

- ⊗ It adds to the problem of e-waste because redundant devices are thrown away.
- ⊗ More devices must be manufactured, with all the associated environmental costs.

Responsible ownership

Responsible use can reduce the environmental impact of digital devices. It involves:

- ✓ keeping devices for longer
- ✓ considering buying a pre-owned device rather than a new one
- ✓ donating unwanted devices to a recycling company or a charity, rather than throwing them away
- ✓ using energy-efficiency measures to reduce power consumption
- ✓ reducing internet usage.

Ways to reduce energy consumption

- Adjust energy settings, such as screen brightness and 'sleep' mode.
- Switch off Bluetooth, Wi-Fi and GPS when not in use.
- Close dormant applications, so that they do not continue to run in the background.

- Disconnect peripherals when not in use.
- When buying a new device, choose one with a high energy-efficiency rating.
- Locate energy-hungry data centres in locations where they can use renewable energy.

Positive impact

Digital technology can help the environment. For example:

- Intelligent traffic control systems keep traffic moving and reduce fuel consumption.

- 'Smart lighting' switches off lights when they are not needed.
- Environmental monitoring ensures that regulations are being followed and prevents poaching and other illegal activities.

Worked example

Target grade 4-6

Explain **one** positive impact that the use of digital technology can have on the environment.

(2 marks)

Using the internet to work from home reduces greenhouse gas emissions because there is less traffic on the road.

Now try this

Target grade 4-6

The world's data centres consume huge amounts of energy.

Describe **two** ways in which the environmental impact of data centres can be reduced.

(4 marks)

Personal data

Personal data is information that relates to a known individual or one whose identify can be deduced. It includes a person's name, passport number, fingerprints, ethnicity, medical record, shopping history and political opinions.

Digital footprint

A digital footprint is the trail of personal data left behind each time someone uses the internet. It includes the websites they visit, emails they send and information they post on social media.

People also give away personal information about themselves while carrying out day-to-day activities, such as paying for a coffee with a bank card, using Google Maps to get directions or making a doctor's appointment. The movements of mobile phone users are tracked as they move between phone masts.

Third parties, including advertisers, health professionals, planners, prospective employers and law enforcement officers collect and use personal data.

 Links There's more about data protection legislation on page 60.

Benefits and drawbacks

The collection and use of personal data has a number of benefits and drawbacks:

- ✓ **Personalisation:** offers can be tailored to an individual's preferences and location.
- ✓ **Convenience:** personal details, such as credit card numbers and addresses, only need to be entered once.
- ✗ **Privacy:** it is not always obvious who is collecting and analysing personal data and who they are passing it on to.
- ✗ **Security:** data breaches occur frequently. If personal data falls into the wrong hands it might be misused.
- ✗ **Discrimination:** analysis of shared data could result in some groups or individuals being discriminated against.
- ✗ **Civil liberties:** analysis of shared data by police forces could wrongly associate innocent people with criminal behaviour or categorise people politically.

Owning the data

There are **ethical issues** linked to the ownership of data and who can use it. These include:

When someone posts a photo on a social media site, they retain the IP, but the company has the right to do what it wants with the photo.	Users will always own their names and addresses, but it is less clear who owns the data about their activity while visiting a website.
Medical records are not the patient's property. In the UK, they belong to the National Health Service. Patients only have a right to view them.	Online retailers sell shoppers' purchase data to other retailers. Google sells people's search histories.

The Data Protection Act 2018 has strict rules about the collection and use of personal data.

Worked example

Target grade 4-6

Explain **two** reasons a person may be concerned about the privacy of their personal data.   **(4 marks)**

1 They may be concerned that their data may not be stored securely, which means it could be stolen and used by cybercriminals.

2 They may be concerned that they will be targeted with unwanted advertisements because their data has been sold on without their consent.

Now try this

Target grade 4-6

Explain **one** benefit to society of collecting and analysing people's personal data on a large scale.   **(3 marks)**

Legislation

Legislation regulates the collection and use of personal data and protects against misuse.

Data Protection Act 2018 (DPA)

Many organisations, including the government, the National Health Service, social networking sites and online retailers, store personal details. The DPA defines a set of principles that organisations must adhere to.

Principle	Organisations must do the following
Lawfulness, fairness and transparency	Have a legitimate reason for processing a person's data, must tell them what they will use the data for and must get their consent.
Purpose limitation	Only use the data for the specific purpose for which it was collected.
Data minimisation	Only collect as much data as is necessary for the specified purpose.
Accuracy	Ensure that the data they collect is accurate and current. When notified of an error in the data, they must update it promptly.
Storage limitation	Not keep data for longer than is necessary.
Security	Keep data secure and protect it against loss or damage.
Accountability	Demonstrate that their data protection measures are adequate.

Anyone whose data is stored is a **data subject**. The DPA gives data subjects the right to:

- be informed about the collection and use of their data
- access their data
- have inaccurate data corrected
- have data erased
- object to how their data is processed
- withdraw consent at any time
- restrict the way in which their data is processed
- obtain and reuse their data for their own purposes
- complain to the Information Commissioner.

Computer misuse

The **Computer Misuse Act 1990** is used to prosecute cybercriminals in the UK. The act identifies three offences:

1. **Unauthorised access to computer material.** This includes logging into another person's computer without their permission.
2. **Unauthorised access with intent to commit further offences.** This includes stealing somebody else's credit card details and using them to commit another crime.
3. **Unauthorised access with intent to impair the running of a computer or to damage or destroy data.** This includes planting a virus or installing malware.

Cookies

A cookie is a small text file that is downloaded onto a user's computer when they visit a website. It enables the website to recognise the user's device and store their preferences.

The **Privacy and Electronic Communications Regulations 2003** govern the use of cookies.

- If a website uses cookies, it must display a message telling users this and get their consent.
- Users can opt out of having data about them collected in this way.

Now try this   Target grade 4-6

The Computer Misuse Act has been updated several times since it first became law in 1990.

Give **one** reason why updates have been necessary. **(1 mark)**

Artificial intelligence (AI)

Artificial intelligence (AI) affects our lives in many different ways. While the use of AI has obvious benefits, it also raises a number of important ethical and legal issues.

Artificial intelligence

AI is the general term for computer systems that are capable of performing tasks that typically require human intelligence, such as pattern recognition, decision making and problem solving.

Machine learning

Machine learning is a subset of AI. Machine-learning algorithms learn by looking for rules and patterns in real-time data. They get pro-gressively better at carrying out tasks, without having specific rules set out in their programs.

Narrow AI

Machine-learning systems are designed to perform a single task or a limited range of tasks. They cannot transfer their knowledge to another type of task and fail when they encounter a situation that falls outside the 'problem space' they were designed to work in. This type of AI is classed as **narrow AI**.

Examples of narrow AI

- email spam filters
- social media monitoring tools
- facial and fingerprint recognition systems
- content recommendations
- voice recognition in digital assistants
- self-driving cars
- lethal autonomous weapons systems.

Robots are programmable machines that interact with the physical world via sensors and actuators. Some are controlled by AI programs that enable them to perform complex tasks.

Algorithmic bias

There is growing recognition that some AI algorithms are **biased**. This results in them making prejudiced decisions that discriminate against certain individuals.

Algorithmic bias can occur because:

- the dataset used to train the AI system is itself biased
- there is a design flaw in the AI algorithm causing it to exaggerate bias rather than ignore it
- the developers who design and build AI systems unintentionally incorporate their own prejudices and preconceptions into them.

Responsibility

The 'black-box' nature of such systems makes it difficult to determine who is **accountable** when an AI system goes wrong. Problems might be the fault of:

- the **creator of the algorithm** – an error in the algorithm may produce unpredictable behaviour or cause the machine to malfunction
- the **supplier of the data** used to train the algorithm – a small or biased set of sample data will result in errors
- the **user of the algorithm** – if they choose to overrule the actions taken by the machine or fail to exercise judgement.

Worked example

Target grade **4-6**

One problem with the voice recognition software used by digital assistants is that it can be confused by background noise. Describe how machine learning can help overcome this problem. **(3 marks)**

Over time, a machine-learning system learns to differentiate a human voice from background noise and to recognise command words.

Now try this

Target grade **4-6**

A multinational company uses a machine-learning algorithm to shortlist applicants for software developer jobs. Despite there being no shortage of excellent female applicants, none are shortlisted by the algorithm. Explain how this could happen. **(2 marks)**

Protecting intellectual property 1

Intellectual property (IP) is a unique creation of the human mind, such as an invention, a computer program, or a graphic image. IP is protected by the Copyright Designs and Patent Act 1988.

Copyright

Copyright protects things, such as novels, textbooks, computer programs, images, films and music recordings.

Copyright protection is automatic. There is no need to register or pay a fee. The creator of a unique work holds the copyright for it.

The copyright holder has the right to publish, copy, distribute and sell the work. No one else can use it without permission. Copyright lasts for 70 years after the death of the copyright holder.

The © symbol indicates that an artefact is copyrighted. Copyright protects the expression of an idea, but not the idea itself.

Licensing

The copyright holder of a work can grant a **licence** that permits a third party to use it. A software licence is a legally binding contract that specifies how software can be used.

- A **Creative commons licence** permits others to use, build upon and distribute the work, providing they adhere to certain conditions.
- An **Attribution-non-commercial licence** allows work to be used, distributed and copied for non-commercial purposes, providing the creator is given credit for having created it.
- An **Attribution commercial licence** allows the same rights and commercial use.
- Work in the **public domain** means that it can be used without permission or attribution for any purpose.

Patents

Patents protect new inventions – both what they do and how they work.

Patent protection is not automatic. It has to be applied for. The applicant has to demonstrate that their invention is different from anything else that exists. A patent holder has the exclusive right to make, use and sell the invention for 20 years.

Disadvantages of patents

Patents and copyright are meant to foster innovation, but may have the opposite effect.
Companies such as Apple, Google and Microsoft, spend vast amounts of money fighting legal battles over patents, money that might be better spent on research and development.

Trademarks

Unique company logos, strap lines, colours and words can all be registered as trademarks.
The ® symbol denotes a trademark that has been officially registered. The ™ symbol denotes one that has not been registered.
Companies use trademarks to distinguish their goods and services from those of their competitors and to protect their brand.
Registration of a trademark lasts for 10 years.

Worked example

Target grade 4-6

Give **two** reasons a company may decide to register and use a trademark to protect its logo. **(2 marks)**

So that the company can:
- take legal action against anyone who uses its logo without permission
- put the ® symbol next to its logo to indicate ownership.

Now try this

Target grade 4-6

Mandeep is a software developer. He has developed a new mobile phone app.

Describe **two** ways Mandeep can protect his intellectual property. **(4 marks)**

Protecting intellectual property 2

Computer users can choose between open-source and proprietary software. Anyone can access and modify the code of open-source software. However, proprietary software is closed-source. No one apart from the copyright holder is permitted to view or modify the code.

Open-source software

Software that is distributed with a licence that allows anyone to use, view, modify and share its source code.

Key features:

- ✓ Users have access to the source code.
- ✓ Users can modify and distribute the software.
- ✓ The software can be installed on any number of machines at the same time.
- ✓ Support is provided by a community of enthusiasts.
- ✓ Most is free to use (there are some exceptions).
- ✗ May not be free of bugs or fully tested.
- ✗ May need specialist knowledge to install.

Examples: LibreOffice, Linux, Android, Firefox, Apache.

Google's mobile Android operating system, which is installed on more than 85% of the world's mobile phones, is a modified version of the open-source Linux operating system. More than 15 000 programmers around the world helped to develop Linux. In contrast, Microsoft Windows was developed by a single company.

Proprietary software

Software that is owned by an individual or a company. Its source code is protected by copyright law, making it illegal for users to modify or share it.

Key features:

- ✓ Thoroughly tested by developers prior to release.
- ✓ Supported by a dedicated team of developers employed by the copyright owner.
- ✓ Should any vulnerabilities or bugs emerge after release, a patch will be developed speedily to solve the problem.
- ✓ Extensive support from third parties (e.g. books, magazines and online tutorials).
- ✗ Users do not have access to the source code, as only an executable file is distributed.
- ✗ Users are not given permission to modify the software, as it is protected by copyright.
- ✗ Usually paid for and licensed on a per-user, per-machine basis.

Examples: Microsoft Windows, iTunes, MacOS, Adobe Photoshop.

Worked example

Target grade 4-6

Annette purchases a proprietary software licence.

List **five** conditions of use that will be specified in the licence agreement.   **(5 marks)**

- The number of computers the software can be installed on.
- How many people can use the software at the same time.
- How long the licence is valid.
- Which settings the software can be used in (educational, commercial, private, etc.).
- Whether the user must agree to allow automatic updates.

Now try this

Target grade 4-6

A school has decided to install an open-source software package on all the computers on its network.

Describe **two** benefits that doing this will provide to the school.   **(4 marks)**

Threats to digital systems 1

A **cyberattack** is a malicious attempt by a **hacker** to gain unauthorised access to a digital system in order to cause damage or steal data.

Malware

Malware is a general term for **malicious software**. Some hackers have the technical skills and ability to write their own malware, but most use code downloaded from the internet.

Typically, a digital device becomes infected by malware when users click on an attachment they are tricked into opening or when they follow a link to a seemingly harmless website.

Reasons hackers use malware	How it works
To infect a computer with a virus or worm. This can cause the computer to run slowly or crash, or can damage/delete data stored on its hard drive.	A **virus** inserts itself into another program and lies hidden waiting for its 'host' to be run. Once activated, a virus makes copies of itself and attaches these to other programs. Infected programs are passed on via email, messaging and social media. **Worms** infect systems by moving from one device to another. They can infect an entire network quickly. Unlike viruses, they do not embed themselves within other programs. They distribute themselves independently of users.
To gain backdoor access into a computer or network and then launch a ransomware attack, harvest sensitive data or hijack a webcam.	A **Trojan** masquerades as legitimate software that users are tricked into downloading. It runs every time the computer is switched on, providing the hacker with access to files stored on the hard drive and a backdoor into devices on the same network. Trojans are used to deliver **ransomware** that encrypts the files on the computer. The victim must pay a ransom in order to get the key to decrypt them.
To spy on what a user is doing.	A **keylogger** secretly records the keystrokes a user makes, enabling the hacker to extract valuable information, such as passwords and credit card numbers.
To create a botnet to carry out distributed denial of service attacks (DDS).	It is easy for hackers to make unsecured **Internet of Things** (IoT) devices (such as security cameras, fitness trackers and baby monitors) part of a **botnet**, an army of zombie devices used to carry out mass attacks. A DDS attack floods a network or website with huge volumes of traffic causing it to crash.

Worked example   Target grade 4-6

The growing use of smart devices in the home is providing opportunities for hackers to launch cyberattacks. Explain **one** reason why this is the case. **(3 marks)**

Many Internet of Things devices are despatched from the factory with a default password set. If the purchaser does not change the password, then a hacker can gain access to the device using a simple script.

Types of hacker

Most hackers are cybercriminals. They are known as **black-hat hackers**. They break into digital systems in order to cause harm. However, some are **white-hat hackers**, who help organisations strengthen their defences against cyberattacks.

Now try this   Target grade 1-3

State **three** types of disruption a malware attack can cause. **(3 marks)**

Threats to digital systems 2

A **technical vulnerability** is a hardware, software or configuration fault that makes it easier for a hacker to attack. Such a fault is known as a **security hole**.

Technical vulnerabilities that hackers exploit

Unpatched software	Hackers exchange information with one another about known security vulnerabilities in software applications. They target these weaknesses in cyberattacks.
	When a security flaw is discovered in software that has been released, the software producer must work quickly to produce a **patch** that will fix the issue.
	A **zero-day vulnerability** is one that is newly discovered and for which no patch has been produced. Once it becomes known, hackers will try to exploit it by launching a **zero-day attack**.
Out-of-date anti-malware	The best defence against malware is **anti-malware** software. This works by scanning files and comparing their contents with a database of known **malware signatures**.
	Anti-malware software only works if its signature library is kept up to date. If that is not the case, recent malware signatures will not be in its library and such malware will be missed. **Links** You can read more about anti-malware on page 42.
Open ports	Services that rely on the internet, such as web browsers, websites and file transfer utilities, use dedicated computer ports to receive and transmit information.
	Hackers can find out which software and services are running on a computer using a technique called **port scanning**, helping them to identify possible attack targets.
Default admin passwords	Some hardware devices, such as routers, modems and file servers, are shipped with factory-set admin passwords. Hackers can look up default passwords on the web and use password-hacking software to crack weak passwords.

Links You can read more about hackers on pages 55 and 64.

Worked example

Alex has set the operating system on his laptop to automatically download and install updates. Explain why this is good practice. **(4 marks)**

Software producers periodically issue updates (patches). This is done to address security flaws that have come to light since the software was first released and to combat any new forms of attack that have emerged. By choosing to install the upgrades automatically, Alex will be certain that his level of protection remains up to date. This will minimise the risk of his laptop becoming infected by malware.

Now try this

Target grade **4-6**

Despite having anti-malware installed, Alex's laptop is infected by a virus. Explain **one** reason why this might have happened. **(2 marks)**

Threats to digital systems 3

Some hackers use **social engineering** techniques to make people reveal confidential information or install harmful software on their computers. Social engineering exploits human nature.

Social engineering techniques and how they work

Phishing	Victims receive an email from a seemingly reputable source. This asks them to click on a link to what appears to be a genuine website, but which is actually controlled by the hacker. Once on the website, the victim is asked to enter their ID and password or credit card details. This confidential information is then harvested by the attacker. Most phishing messages are sent as bulk mailings that target thousands of potential victims, at least some of whom will be fooled.
Pretexting (blagging)	The hacker pretends to be from a trusted organisation that is known to the victim. The hacker says that there is an emergency that must be dealt with. By stressing the urgency of the situation, the attacker panics the victim into divulging confidential information.
Baiting	Victims are offered a free giveaway, such as a music download or a movie preview. This giveaway comes bundled with harmful malware which infects the victim's computer. A hacker may also leave USB memory sticks infected with malware lying around for victims to find. If someone takes the bait and plugs one of the sticks into their computer, then it will be infected.
Quid pro quo	Victims provide their login details and other security information in exchange for a service, such as a free software upgrade or enhanced virus protection. The attacker offers to help with the setup and installation. This gives them an opportunity to install malware.
Shoulder-surfing	The hacker looks over a victim's shoulder, uses binoculars to watch from a distance, or uses a camera to note their login name, password, PIN, etc.

Worked example

Target grade 1-3

Sienna receives a security notification that says it is from her bank. It asks her to click on a link to change her password. She thinks it may be a phishing attempt.

List **three** reasons why Sienna might be suspicious. **(3 marks)**

- The notification is poorly written and has spelling mistakes.
- She is asked to click on a link.
- It says that the situation is urgent and requires an immediate response.

Other indications that the email may not be genuine include:

- there is a suspicious attachment
- the email address does not look genuine
- it uses a generic greeting, such as 'Dear Customer', rather than the recipient's name.

Now try this

Target grade 1-3

A hacker uses social engineering techniques to persuade people to divulge confidential information about themselves.

Give **two** ways in which the attacker could use this information for financial gain. **(2 marks)**

Protecting digital systems 1

There are a number of measures that can protect digital systems and data from cyberattacks. **Defence-in-depth** involves using a combination of defence mechanisms, so that, if an attacker gets around one obstacle, they meet another and then another.

Firewall

A firewall is the first line of defence for a networked device. It acts as a barrier between the internal network and the internet, monitoring incoming and outgoing traffic. Firewalls use a pre-defined set of rules to determine what to allow through from one side to the other.

Firewalls also spot suspicious activity within networks, such as users who try to visit harmful websites or who download files from file-sharing sites.

Links There is more about firewalls on page 56.

Anti-malware software

The best defence against malware is **anti-malware** software. Traditional anti-malware works by scanning files and comparing their contents with a library of known **malware signatures**. If any of the signature patterns are found in the file, it is quarantined until the user decides whether to let it in or delete it.

New malware is being released all the time, so this type of anti-malware becomes out of date unless its signature database is refreshed.

Links See page 65 for more about the problems of out-of-date anti-malware.

More sophisticated software uses **heuristic analysis** to look for suspicious behaviours that could indicate a new form of malware or a modified version of a known threat.

Static heuristic analysis compares the source code of the suspicious file with that of known malware. If enough of the code matches, the file is identified as malware.

Dynamic heuristic analysis isolates the suspicious file inside a virtual machine (sandbox) to test what would happen if it was allowed to run. Each command is examined as it is executed to identify any suspicious actions.

Encryption

While encrypting data will not prevent it from being stolen, it does protect its **confidentiality**. Encryption is the process of converting data into a scrambled format that is not understandable. Only an authorised person, who has the **key** needed to **decrypt** it, can read and understand it.

There are two forms of encryption. **Symmetric encryption** uses the same key to both encrypt and decrypt the data. **Asymmetric encryption** uses two different keys – a public key to encrypt the data and a private key, which only the recipient knows, to decrypt it.

Worked example
Target grade **4-6**

Describe **one** reason asymmetric encryption is more secure than symmetric encryption. **(4 marks)**

Symmetric encryption uses one key which is shared by both the sender and recipient. There is a chance that the key could be intercepted in transit. In asymmetric encryption, a private key, known only to the recipient, is used to decrypt the data. This means there is less possibility of it being stolen.

Now try this
Target grade **4-6**

An organisation has set up a WAN linking its sites throughout the country.

Explain **two** measures the organisation should take to protect its network and data from attack. **(4 marks)**

Protecting digital systems 2

An organisation's systems and data must be protected from a wide range of threats, including natural disasters, technical failures and the accidental or malicious actions of employees.

Backup and recovery procedures

Having a backup and recovery procedure will not protect an organisation's data from loss or damage, but it will enable it to be recovered if the worst happens.

Backing up involves making a copy of the data and storing it on a different device in a different location, offsite or in the cloud.

Recovery is the process of restoring data and/or system states from the backup copy. Recovery plans may include arrangements for relocating staff and equipment to an alternative site.

Backing up is often automated. Two common approaches are:

- **Full backup** – a full copy is made of all the data, regardless of whether it has been changed since the last backup.
- **Incremental backup** – copies new files and those changed since the last backup.

RAID

One commonly used approach to backing up is RAID. The contents of each hard disk on a server are replicated on a second disk. Should one disk fail, the other springs into action, allowing the failed disk to be swapped out without the server having to be shut down.

Acceptable use policy (AUP)

Social engineering relies on people being tricked into behaving foolishly or making mistakes. The best tool an organisation can use to reduce this risk is an AUP.

An AUP is a collection of rules and procedures that users are required to follow. It spells out what constitutes appropriate and inappropriate behaviour. It also states the actions that will be taken if a user disregards the policy.

Examples of appropriate behaviour:

- Log off or lock the screen before leaving a computer unattended.
- Use a secure password and do not disclose it to others.
- Exercise caution when opening email attachments.

Examples of inappropriate behaviour:

- Install software downloaded from the web.
- Plug a memory stick into a USB slot.
- Give out confidential information over the phone or in an email.
- Remove data from the premises without authority.
- Access social media sites in work time.

Users must sign a copy of the AUP to acknowledge that they have read it and agree to abide by it. Training is often provided to reinforce the AUP.

Worked example

Target grade 4-6

Give **two** reasons an organisation should have an AUP. **(2 marks)**

- It makes users aware of what is and is not acceptable behaviour.
- It stops them wasting time and network bandwidth on personal activities.

Having an AUP will help an organisation meet its legal liability to keep personal data secure because its users will be better informed about the dangers of hacking. They will be more likely to recognise an attempt by hackers to trick them into revealing confidential information.

Now try this

Target grade 4-6

1 State **two** advantages of making an incremental backup rather than a full backup. **(2 marks)**
2 Explain **one** disadvantage of doing this. **(3 marks)**

Problem-solving
with programming

Decomposition and abstraction

Computer scientists use computational thinking skills to define and analyse problems, design structured algorithmic solutions, and translate algorithms into a form that can be executed in a computer.

> **Links** Decomposition and abstraction are two computational thinking skills. You can find out more on page 1.

Problem statement

You may be presented with a **problem statement** such as:

> A program is needed to report the mean of a set of numbers entered by the user.
> Only positive numbers can be entered. The mean must be reported to two decimal places.

Decomposition

The first step is to read the problem statement carefully and break it down into smaller parts. Try identifying inputs, processes and outputs.

- Input – positive numbers.
- Processing – calculating mean.
- Output – the mean.

Abstraction

The second step is to determine what you can ignore and what you need to know.

- Need to check for negative numbers.
- Ignore any other data type input.
- Need to know how to format decimals.

Implement abstraction

To implement the abstraction, fill in the gaps between the comments.

Expressing abstractions

One of the best ways to express a solution abstraction is with comments. You can do this even before you write any code.

```
1    # All the global variables
2    numIn = -1
3    total = 0
4    count = 0
5    layout = "Mean: {:6.2f}"
6
7    # Get the input
8    numIn = int (input ("Enter a number "))
9
10   # Keep looping as long as valid input
11   while (numIn >= 0):
12       # Track items for calculation
13       total = total + numIn
14       count = count + 1
15
16       # Get another input
17       numIn = int (input ("Enter a number "))
18
19   # Print the outputs
20   if (count > 0):
21       print (layout.format (total / count))
```

> You can find out more about formatting output on pages 84 and 85.

> You can see the decompositions of:
> - input (line 8)
> - processing (line 13)
> - output (line 21).

> You can see the abstractions checking for valid numbers (line 11) and using the formatting functionality (line 5).

> If count was 0, then the program would crash.

Now try this

Target grade 7-9

A program is needed to print out the times tables (1 to 12) for any number entered by the user. The program should print out the times tables until the user signals it to stop by entering a 0. The output should be on a single line. For example: 2 4 6 8 10 12 14 16 18 20 22 24.

Decompose the problem. Abstract away unwanted detail and identify the important points.

Create a solution abstraction by using comments only. Complete the program by providing code for the comments. Test your program to ensure it works with all anticipated inputs. **(5 marks)**

Read, analyse and refine programs

When approaching a coding problem you will need to read, analyse and refine the code you are given. Refine means to change a program in some way. When writing or refining code, you need to meet a set of requirements. These include requirements for best practice or efficiency.

Worked example

Target grade 1-3

Here is a program that checks a number to see which of four ranges it falls into. Amend the code to check the data using a more efficient method. **(3 marks)**

```
1    import random
2
3    number = 0
4
5    number = random.randint (1, 100)
6    print ("The number is", number)
7
8    if (number < 10):
9        print ("Too small")
10   if (number >= 10) and (number <= 50)
11       print ("Lower side")
12   if (number > 50) and (number <= 80)
13       print ("Higher side")
14   if (number > 80) and (number <= 100)
15       print ("Too high")
```

First you need to **read** and **analyse** this code. You can see that any single number can only be in one of the ranges. However, the code is using four different **if** statements. That means all four range tests are being executed for each number. For example, if the number is 5, it is still checked for being in the 10–50 range, the 51–80 range and the 81–100 range. This is inefficient.

Now you need to **refine** the code to improve its efficiency. The fact that any single number can only be in one of the ranges means that an if…elif…elif…else statement can be used. Replacing multiple if statements with a single if…elif…elif…else statement means that if any test is true, the remaining tests are not executed.

Sample answer

```
1    import random
2
3    number = 0
4
5    number = random.randint (1, 100)
6    print ("The number is", number)
7
8    if (number < 10):
9        print ("Too small")
10   elif (number <= 50)
11       print ("Lower side")
12   elif (number <= 80)
13       print ("Higher side")
14   else:
15       print ("Too high")
```

Now try this

Target grade 4-6

Here is a program that sums seven numbers.

Analyse the code to identify a more efficient way to store the data. Amend the code to:

- store the data using a more efficient method
- process the data stored using the more efficient method. **(3 marks)**

 .PY See Read, analyse and refine programs Student.py

```
1    total = 0
2    var1 = 11
3    var2 = 22
4    var3 = 33
5    var4 = 44
6    var5 = 55
7    var6 = 66
8    var7 = 77
9
10   total = var1 + var2 + var3 + \
11          var4 + var5 + var6 + var 7
12
13   print (total)
```

The '\' character in Python allows you to break long lines so they fit on the page.

Convert algorithms 1

After designing an algorithm and expressing it in a flowchart, you must convert it to Python code. The logic of flowchart symbols can be translated to Python, but it is not always a one-to-one relationship. On this page you will revise converting sequence, input and output from flowcharts to Python.

 Links   You can find out more about the use of sequence, input, and output in flowcharts on page 3.

Sequence

Sequence means an ordered set of instructions. It is represented by the arrows in a flowchart. It is translated into Python by placing **one instruction after another.**

Start and stop

There is no specific Python instruction for the start and stop flowchart symbols. A program starts when it begins running and stops when the last instruction is executed.

Input and output

Input and output symbols, representing keyboard input and display output, are translated into Python by using the input() and print() functions.

Devices

Different input and output devices may use other functions, such as readline() and write() for files. These might appear in a process symbol.

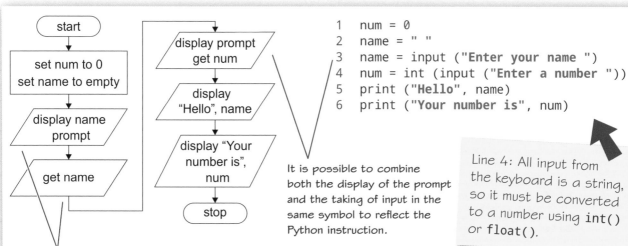

```
1   num = 0
2   name = " "
3   name = input ("Enter your name ")
4   num = int (input ("Enter a number "))
5   print ("Hello", name)
6   print ("Your number is", num)
```

It is possible to combine both the display of the prompt and the taking of input in the same symbol to reflect the Python instruction.

Line 4: All input from the keyboard is a string, so it must be converted to a number using int() or float().

Using flowchart symbols, the printing of the display can be shown separately to the taking of the input.

Now try this

Target grade 1-3

This flowchart is for an algorithm that performs some simple arithmetic.

Write the code to implement the algorithm in the flowchart. Do **not** add any additional functionality. **(10 marks)**

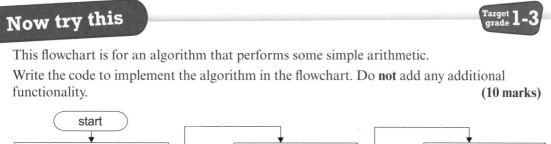
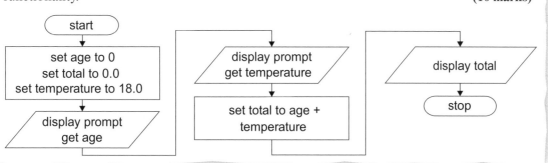

Problem-solving with programming

Convert algorithms 2

Most algorithms use decision making of some kind to select alternative paths through code. This is **selection**. The choice of path is based on a test condition. Selection is translated into Python using the **if…elif…else** statement. On this page you will revise converting selection from flowcharts to Python.

🔗 **Links** You can find out more about the use of selection in flowcharts on page 4.

Target grade 4-6

Worked example

Here is a flowchart for an algorithm that displays a message depending on the number input.

Write the code to implement the algorithm in the flowchart. Do **not** add any additional functionality.

(7 marks)

```
set num to 0
        ↓
display prompt
get num
        ↓
is num less than 1?  ──no──▶  is num greater than 10?  ──no──▶  display "Just right"
        │ yes                         │ yes
        ▼                             ▼
display "Too small"          display "Too large"
```

> When the flowchart has symbols on the 'no' path, you will need an **else**. When the flowchart has multiple selection symbols in a row, you need to check if it requires an **elif**.

Sample answer

```
1    num = 0
2    num = int (input ("Enter a number"))
3    if (num < 1):
4        print ("Too small")
5    elif (num > 10):
6        print ("Too large")
7    else
8        print ("Just right")
```

◀ There are two selection symbols in a row, so the first converts to an **if** and the second converts to an **elif**.

◀ The 'Just right' message is on the 'no' path of a selection, so it goes under **else**.

Now try this

Target grade 4-6

Here is a flowchart for an algorithm that determines where a student will sit for a school assembly.

Write the code to implement the algorithm in the flowchart. Do **not** add any additional functionality.

(7 marks)

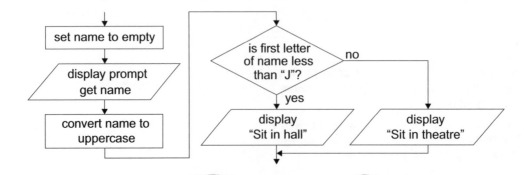

```
set name to empty
        ↓
display prompt
get name
        ↓
convert name to uppercase
        ↓
is first letter of name less than "J"?  ──no──▶  display "Sit in theatre"
        │ yes
        ▼
display "Sit in hall"
```

Problem-solving with programming

Convert algorithms 3

Algorithms commonly need to repeat the same code multiple times as long as a condition is true. This is a condition-controlled loop. **Condition-controlled repetition** is translated into Python using the **while** statement. On this page you will revise converting condition-controlled repetition from flowcharts to Python.

> **Links** You can find out more about the use of condition-controlled repetition in flowcharts on page 5.

Worked example

Target grade 1-3

Here is a flowchart for an algorithm that displays a message depending on the number input.

Write the code to implement the algorithm in the flowchart. Do **not** add any additional functionality. **(7 marks)**

> The loop is indicated by the backward arrow to the top of the selection symbol. It is a condition-controlled loop because the number of times around the loop is not known when the loop starts.

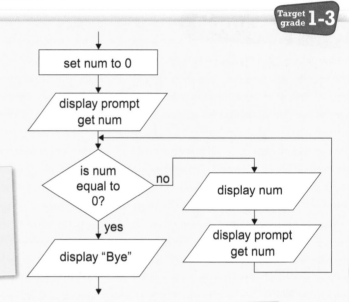

Sample answer

```
1    num = 0
2
3    num = int (input ("Enter a number"))
4    while (num != 0):
5        print (num)
6        num = int (input ("Enter a number"))
7
8    print ("Bye")
```

> The outcome of the test is dependent on an unknown user input.

> You must recognise that using a loop (backward arrow) with a condition that Is not controlled by a counter can be translated as a **while** statement.

Now try this

Target grade 1-3

Here is a flowchart for an algorithm that simulates the repeated playing of a game.

Write the code to implement the algorithm in the flowchart. Do **not** add any additional functionality. **(7 marks)**

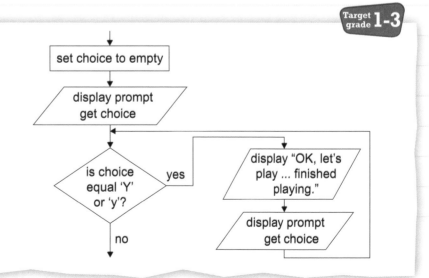

Convert algorithms 4

Another type of repetition is carried out for a fixed number of times. This is a count-controlled loop. **Count-controlled repetition** is translated into Python using the **for in range** statement. On this page you will revise converting count-controlled repetition from flowcharts to Python.

 Links You can find out more about the use of count-controlled repetition in flowcharts on page 5.

Worked example

 Target grade 4-6

Here is a flowchart for a 1-2-3-go algorithm.

Write the code to implement the algorithm in the flowchart. Do **not** add any additional functionality.

(4 marks)

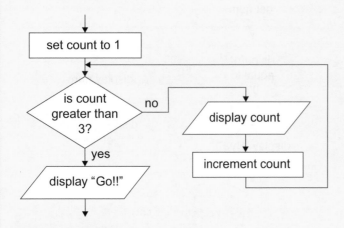

The loop is indicated by the backward arrow that points to the top of the selection symbol.

It is a count-controlled loop because the number of times around the loop is known before the loop starts (in this case three times).

Sample answer

```
1   for count in range (1, 4):
2       print (count)
3
4   print ("Go!!")
```

You must recognise that using a loop (backward arrow) with either an increment or decrement to a counter can be translated as a **for…in range()** statement in Python.

Now try this

Target grade 4-6

Here is a flowchart for an algorithm that implements a countdown from 10.

Write the code to implement the algorithm in the flowchart.

Do **not** add any additional functionality.

(5 marks)

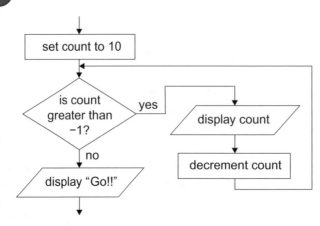

The numbers generated by the **range()** function in Python include the bottom number but not the top number. It can also generate numbers in reverse by using a step value of −1.

Convert algorithms 5

The final type of loop used in algorithms executes the same action on every item in a data structure. This is known as iteration. **Iteration through a data structure** is translated into Python using the **for…in** statement. This is sometimes referred to as a for each loop. On this page you will revise converting iteration from flowcharts to Python.

> 🔗 **Links**   You can find out more about the use of iteration in flowcharts on page 6.

Worked example

Target grade **4-6**

Here is a flowchart for an algorithm that displays types of mushrooms.

Write the code to implement the algorithm in the flowchart. Do **not** add any additional functionality.

(10 marks)

> The loop is indicated by the backward arrow pointing to the top of the selection symbol. The number of times through the loop is known (the length of the list).

Flowchart:
- set list to "morcel", "shiitake", "porcini", "oyster"
- any mushrooms left unprocessed? → no
- yes → display mushroom
- next mushroom

Sample answer

```
1   mushroomList = ["morel", "shiitake",
2                   "porcini", "oyster"]
3
4   for mushroom in mushroomList:
5       print (mushroom)
```

> You must recognise that using a loop (backward arrow) with an indication of a 'next' item, can be translated as a for…in statement in Python.

Now try this

Target grade **4-6**

Here is a flowchart for an algorithm that generates a list of random numbers and then processes the list.

Write the code to implement the algorithm in the flowchart.

Do **not** add any additional functionality.

(10 marks)

Import the random library and use a count-controlled repetition to fill the list with integers.

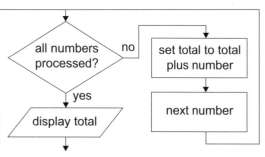

Flowchart:
- set numList to empty list / set total to 0
- fill numList with 100 random integers between 100 and 500, inclusive
- all numbers processed? → no → set total to total plus number → next number
- yes → display total

Readability

It is important to ensure your program's logic is clear and easy to understand so that it is easier for others to maintain the code. This is useful as programs are often developed by teams. Readability is important. If your logic is difficult to see, it may not be recognised by examiners.

Techniques for making programs easy to read

- Lay out your code into sections for: libraries, constants, global variables and subprograms. These should be separated from the main program.
- Use comments to explain your logic by section, not by line.
- Create meaningful identifiers for variables and subprograms (given the context of the problem).
- Use white space to separate blocks of code by functionality.

Indentation

Indentation is part of the Python syntax. Your editor may insert it automatically, but check that it matches your intended logic.

Worked example

Target grade 1-3

This program displays the mean of a list of numbers. Amend the code using a range of techniques to make it more readable. **(7 marks)**

```
1    a = 0
2    b = [55, 22, 88, 99, 33]
3    a = len (b)
4    s = 0
5    for i in b:
6        s = s + i
7    x = 0.0
8    x = s / a
9    print (s,x)
```

Sample answer

```
1    # Global variables
2    myList = [55, 22, 88, 99, 33]
3    length = 0    # Integer
4    total = 0     # Integer
5    mean = 0.0    # Real
6
7    # Loop through the whole list
8    #      adding the numbers
9    for number in myList:
10       total = total + number
11
12   # Calculate the mean
13   length = len (myList)
14   mean = total / length
15
16   # Display the outputs
17   print (total, mean)
```

- Similar instructions (global variables, processing and output) have been grouped together.
- Extra white space has been used to show decomposition of blocks of code.
- Comments have been used effectively to explain the logic in blocks.
- Variable names have been used that make sense in the context of the problem.

Now try this

Target grade 1-3

Here is a program that generates a random number between 1 and 100 (inclusive). The program then checks if the guess is too low, too high or correct. The user is given the option to go again.

Amend the code using a range of techniques to make it more readable. **(7 marks)**

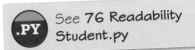 See 76 Readability Student.py

```
1    a = "Y"
2    while (a == "Y"):
3        x = 0
4        import random
5        x = random.randint (1, 100)
6        print ("The number is", x)
7        if (x < 10):
8            print ("Too small")
9        elif (x > 30):
10           print ("Too high")
11       else:
12           print (str (x) + "is perfect")
13       a = input ("Another round?")
```

Program errors

You need to know how to identify and fix errors in code.

 Links   You can find out more about errors in algorithms on page 14.

Syntax errors

Syntax errors are errors in the use of the programming language grammar.

```
1    for count in range (1, 10)
2        print (count
3    IF (index > 10):
4        print ("Count is high")
```

— The ':' is missing.

— A closing ')' is missing.

— The keyword 'if' has been misspelled.

Editors

Syntax errors are usually highlighted in code editors. This makes finding them easier.

Runtime errors

Runtime errors cause programs to crash.
When this happens the interpreter gives an error. It also produces a message that will help you fix the error, for example:

TypeError: unsupported operand type(s) for +: 'int' and 'str'

```
1    myList = [1, 2, 3, 4]
2    newList = []
3    for number in myList:
4        newList.append (number + "A")
```

A 'TypeError' is generated when an integer is added to a string.

Best practice

Runtime errors are difficult to spot until a program is run. Always run your code and check for error messages.

Logic errors

Logic errors produce unintended or unpredictable outcomes.
This program is supposed to add up the numbers 0 to 3 to give a total of 6. However, it outputs the number 3.

```
1    num = 3
2    count = 0
3    total = 0
4
5    while (count < num):
6        total = total + count
7        count = count + 1
8    print (total)
```

A '<' operator is used instead of a '<=' operator.

Best practice

Logic errors are easier to find if you run the code under a debugger in your Integrated Development Environment.

Now try this

Target grade 1-3

Here is a program that displays the colours in a traffic light.

Amend the code to:
- fix one syntax error (line 4)
- fix one runtime error (infinite loop)
- fix one logic error ('green' is not displayed).

(3 marks)

```
1    colours = ["green", "amber", "red"]
2    index = 1
3
4    while (index < len colours)):
5        print (colours[index])
6        index == index + 1
```

Fix the errors in this order, as you cannot run the code with a syntax error in it.

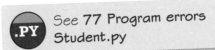 **.PY**   See **77 Program errors Student.py**

Fitness for purpose and efficiency

You must be able to evaluate a program's fitness for purpose and efficiency. You should do this by analysing a program for the number of **compares** and the number of **passes through a loop** it contains and for its use of **memory**. Check to see if multiple variables are used instead of a single list. Check if copies are made of the data during the program.

Worked example

 Links You can find out more about the fitness for purpose and efficiency of algorithms on page 19.

This program finds a target in a list of numbers. It reports if the number is found. Amend the code to make it more efficient. **(4 marks)**

Target grade 4-6

```
1    nums = [23, 13, 7, 3, 6, 16, 5, 11]
2    found = False
3    target = 7
4    for number in nums:
5        if (number == target):
6            print ("Found " + str (target))
7            found = True
8    if (found != True):
9        print (str (target) + " not found.")
```

The loop looks at every item, even if the target has already been found. A 'while' loop would not need to look at every item.

The code could be rewritten to stop looping once the target is found.

Sorting the list before searching and using a while loop means the loop could stop if the program passes the location where the target should be.

Sample answer

```
1    nums = [3, 5, 6, 7, 11, 13, 16, 23]
2    found = False
3    target = 8
4    index = 0
5    passed = False
6    while ((not found) and (not passed) and
7           (index < len (nums))):
8        if (nums[index] == target):
9            print ("Found " + str (target))
10           found = True
11       elif (nums[index] > target):
12           passed = True
13       else:
14           index = index + 1
15   if (found != True):
16       print (str (target) + "not found.")
```

The improved code has sorted the data before the search.

It uses a 'while' loop.

It checks to see if the target location is passed.

More problems

You might also meet problems involving:
- reducing the number of 'if' statements
- using structured data instead of multiple variables
- removing repeated code to reduce the chance of errors.

Now try this

Target grade 4-6

Here is a program that calculates the cost of an order based on how many items are in the order.

Amend the code to make it more efficient.

(4 marks)

Count	Discount
1 to 5	Base rate
6 to 15	80% of base rate
16 or more	70% of base rate

 .PY See 78 Fitness for purpose and efficiency Student.py

```
1    BASE = 36.87
2    count = 0.0
3
4    count = float (input ("Enter a count "))
5    if (count >= 1) and (count <= 5):
6        cost = count * BASE
7        print ("{:4.2f}".format (cost))
8    if (count >= 6) and (count <= 15):
9        cost = count * 0.80 * BASE
10       print ("{:4.2f}".format (cost))
11   if (count >= 16):
12       cost = count * 0.70 * BASE
13       print ("{:4.2f}".format (cost))
```

Structural components of programs

It is important to be able to **identify the structural components** of programs when discussing algorithms.

You must be able to recognise: constants, variables, initialisation and assignment statements, command sequences, selection, repetition, iteration, data structures, subprograms, parameters and input/output.

Identifying components

You can identify a constant because constants are written in all upper case.

```
1    MAX_OCCUPANCY = 6
2
3    numPeople = int ()
4    numPeople = 0
5
6    numPeople = int (input ("Enter number: "))
7    if (numPeople < 1):
8        print ("Invalid number")
9    elif (numPeople > MAX_OCCUPANCY):
10       print ("Too many people")
11   else:
12       print ("Number of people will fit.")
```

This is a declaration of a variable. You can recognise it because it will include a data type.

This is the initialisation of a variable. It is the first time a value is set.

The = is the assignment operator. The input() function is used to take input from the keyboard.

This is selection. It includes all lines from 7 to 12.

The print() function is used to output information.

Some components are made up of more than a single line of code, like the selection in this example.

Now try this

Target grade **1-3**

Here is a program that draws a square with the length of the sides provided by a user.

1 Give the name of a variable.

2 Give the line number of an assignment.

3 Give **three** line numbers that make up a sequence of commands.

4 Give the line number(s) for a repetition.

5 Give the value of a parameter.

(5 marks)

In some Integrated Development Environments (IDEs) you may need to use an instruction to keep the turtle window open once the program ends. Look in the Programming Language Subset document for the turtle functions.

```
1    import turtle
2
3    sideLength = 0
4    tim = turtle.Turtle()
5
6    sideLength = int (input ("Length: "))
7    tim.pencolor ("BlueViolet")
8
9    for numSides in range (4):
10       tim.forward (sideLength)
11       tim.left (90)
```

Iteration

Iteration is needed when the **same actions** are to be **repeated on every single item** in a data structure. It is a kind of loop. It is used when the number of times the loop must be repeated is known.

 Links See pages 6 and 75 for more about iteration.

Using a **for** statement

In Python, iteration is written using the **for** statement. Think of it as being the same as 'for each item in a data structure'.

Extra information is added to indicate the 'times around the loop'. This might be a variable, indicating that 'each' item in a list is to be addressed, or it might be a set of numbers, indicating the indices of the items in the list that must be addressed.

Using a **for... in** statement

```
for <item> in <structure>:
    <command>
```

This executes <command> for each element <item> of a data structure <structure>, in one dimension only.

```
1  numList = [2, 4, 6, 8, 10]
2
3  for num in numList:
4      print (num * 10)
```

The keywords **for** and **in**.

The identifier that changes for each pass through the loop.

The indented command that is executed inside the loop.

Using a **for... in range()** statement

```
for <id> in range (<start>, <stop>, <step>):
    <command>
```

This executes <command> a fixed number of times, based on the numbers generated by the **range()** function, adding <step> each time.

```
1  flowers = ["rose", "tulip", "lilac", "azalea", "peony", "carnation"]
2  theFlower = ""
3  theLetter = ""
4
5  for index in range (0, len (flowers)):
6      theFlower = flowers[index]
7      theLetter = theFlower[0]
8      print ("The first letter of the flower at position " +
9              str (index) + " is " + theLetter)
```

range() generates a set of indices.

Now try this

Target grade **4-6**

A program is required to display the contents of a data structure containing integer numbers. Here is the data structure.

`myList = [1, 2, 3, 4, 5, 6, 7, 8, 9, 10]`

Here is the console output required.

```
1 2 3 4 5 6 7 8 9 10
10 8 6 4 2
```

The program must meet these requirements:

- use a for... in loop to print out the contents of the list
- use a for... in range() loop to print out the even numbers, in reverse order.

Write a program to meet these requirements.

(7 marks)

Repetition

Repetition is needed when an action is to be repeated as long as a condition is true (condition-controlled) or for a fixed number of times (count-controlled). It is a kind of loop.

Using a while statement (condition-controlled loop)

Links   See pages 5, 73 and 74 for more about repetition.

In Python, condition-controlled repetition is written using the **while** statement, with one or more test conditions.

```
while <condition>:
    <command>
```

← This executes <command> as long as <condition> is true.

```
1   choice = 0
2   choice = int (input ("Enter a number, 0 to exit "))
3   while (choice != 0):
4       print ("You entered " + str (choice))
5       choice = int (input ("Enter a number, 0 to exit "))
6
7   print ("You entered 0 – goodbye.")
```

As long as the user does not enter the number 0, the loop will keep going around.

Using a for statement (count-controlled loop)

In Python, count-controlled repetition can be written using the **for** statement and the range() function.

```
for <id> in range (<start>, <stop>, <step>):
    <command>
```

 ← This executes <command> a fixed number of times, based on the numbers generated by the range() function, adding <step> each time.

```
1   total = 0
2   for count in range (0, 10):
3       total = total + count
4       print (count, total)
```

The value of count starts at 0, goes up 1 for each pass of the loop, until it is 9. Recall, counting stops 1 less than the value of <stop>.

Now try this

Target grade 4-6

A program is required to implement a menu system.

The program must meet these requirements:

- menu choices are for sandwiches, biscuits, cake or to quit the program
- accept both upper and lower case for each choice
- keep the user inside the menu system until a valid input is entered
- print a message for the user only when the input is valid.

- Use string operators to control the case of the input.
- Use compound test conditions with Boolean operators.

Write a program to meet these requirements. **(7 marks)**

Structured data types

A data structure is an organised collection of elements. It can be one-dimensional or two-dimensional. Data structures are implemented in Python as **lists**.

 Links You can find out more about data structures on pages 8 and 9 and using iteration with data structures on page 80.

Array

An array is a data structure where all the elements are the same data type. It may be one-dimensional or two-dimensional.

```
1    colourArray = ["DeepPink",
2                   "LemonChiffon",
3                   "CornflowerBlue"]
4    rgbArray = [[255, 20, 147],
5                [255, 250, 205],
6                [100, 149, 237]]
7    for colour in colourArray:
8        print (colour)
9    print (colourArray [1])
10   print (rgbArray[1])
11   print (rgbArray[1][2])
```

Accesses one single element at a time, one after another.

Outputs LemonChiffon, a single element.

Outputs [255, 250, 205], a single element, which itself is an array, as indicated by the square brackets.

Outputs 205. The [1] accesses the array in position 1 and the [2] accesses the single number in position 2 of that array.

To access any data structure, you need one index per dimension.

Records

The elements in a record are of different data types. A single record is a one-dimensional data structure. A group of records is stored in a table. A table is a two-dimensional data structure. Accessing elements in a record works in the same way as it does in an array.

```
1    rgbTable = [["khaki", 240, 230, 140],
2                ["salmon", 250, 128, 114],
3                ["coral", 255, 127, 80]]
4    for colour in rgbTable:
5        print (colour)
6    print (rgbTable[1])
7    print (rgbTable[1][0])
8    for item in rgbTable[2]:
9        print (item)
```

In a two-dimensional data structure, each element in the second dimension can be accessed as a one-dimensional data structure.

Now try this

Target grade 7-9

A program is required to store and display information about the A-series of paper sizes (in millimetres). A0 is 841 × 1189, A1 is 594 × 841, A2 is 420 × 594, A3 is 297 × 420, A4 is 210 × 297, A5 is 148 × 210.

The program must:

- use a two-dimensional table of records to store each paper size name, its width in millimetres, and its length in millimetres
- calculate the area of each paper size
- display the size, width, length and area in a columnar format
- display area information to two decimal places only
- use appropriate column names
- use comments to explain the logic
- use layout to ensure the code is readable and maintainable
- function correctly even if sizes are added to or removed from the series.

Write a program to meet the requirements.   **(10 marks)**

Data types, variables and constants

Variables are named areas in memory that have an associated data type. The **contents** of a variable can change during program execution, but its associated **data type** should not. A named area in memory whose value should not change during execution is a **constant**.

> 🔗 **Links** For more information about these topics, see page 7.

Data types

Each variable and constant has a data type. These include:

- **integer** – whole numbers
- **real or float** – numbers with fractional parts (decimals)
- **Boolean** – values of True or False only
- **string** – values between single or double quotes.

Variables

Memory for variables is allocated when the name and data type is declared. Setting the value in memory for the first time is called **initialisation**.

In Python, the data type can be determined from the value it is assigned first.

Constants

When a value should not change during execution, it is a constant. Constants should be written in **all upper case** (they can include underscores and digits, if required).

Best practice

Using constants reduces the need to change a value in many different places throughout a program. This leads to fewer errors.

Indicating data types, variables and constants

A declaration, which allocates memory and associates a data type.

A declaration of a constant. No value yet assigned.

Creation of a constant with an implicit data type of string.

```
1   myDecimal = float ()
2   myDecimal = 5.23
3   myBoolean = bool ()
4   myBoolean = False
5   MAX_HEIGHT = int ()
6   MAX_HEIGHT = 12
7   STOP = "STOP"
8   theName = "History"
9   theYear = 2019
10  theVolume = 3.589
11  theStatus = False
```

An initialisation to a first value.

An initialisation of a constant to a value.

Data type determined from the first assignment.

Now try this

Target grade 1-3

A program is being developed that creates some variables and displays them. It uses the variables and constants described in the table.

Description	Method of creation
Height in metres, with a decimal	Declare and initialise separately
Number of sweets in a jar	Declare and initialise separately
Whether a car engine is switched on	Declare implicitly and initialise
Name of a shop	Declare implicitly and initialise
Speed limit on a single carriageway	Declare implicitly and initialise
Value of pi to five decimal places	Declare and initialise separately

The program must meet these requirements:

- It must use meaningful identifiers.
- It must initialise each variable and constant to an appropriate value.
- It must display the contents of each item in the main program.

Write the program. Ensure your program works.

(7 marks)

String manipulation

A string is a sequence of characters, made up from those available on the keyboard.

String functions

Python has many **built-in functions** to manipulate strings. See the Programming Language Subset for the full list of the built-in functions that you need to know how to use.

```
1   myString = "When data can't drive, it takes the bus."
2   lengthString = len (myString)
3   print (lengthString)
4
5   position = myString.find ("drive")
6   if (position != -1):
7       print ("Found drive at " + str (position))
8
9   print (myString.upper ())
10  print (myString.lower ())
11
12  myString = "data bus, address bus, control bus"
13  print (myString)
14  print (myString.replace ("bus", "train"))
```

The len() function returns the length of a string.

You can find any substring by using the <string>.find() function. Notice it returns −1 when the substring is not there. Be sure to check for this.

You can convert entire strings to different cases. This is useful to avoid additional checks for variations of case, such as 'Y' or 'y'.

Replacing one substring with another is done with the <string>.replace() function. This may change the length of the original string.

String query functions

Another set of functions allows you to find out about a string.

```
1   thePin = "3065"
2   theInitials = "GTW"
3   theID = "DrS22"
4   theAbbreviation = "etc"
5
6   print (theInitials.isalpha ())
7   print (theID.isalnum ())
8   print (thePin.isdigit ())
9   print (theInitials.isupper ())
10  print (theAbbreviation.islower ())
```

You can find out if a string is all alphabetic characters or a combination of letters and digits.

You can check if the string only holds digits.

You can also find out the case of the string.

Now try this

A program is needed to transform the case of strings, entered from the keyboard. If the string is all lower case, it is transformed to upper case. If the string is all upper case, it is transformed to lower case. Transformed strings should be displayed to the user. If the input is mixed case, the user is told to try again. An empty string terminates the program. A console session is shown on the right.

Write a program that meets these requirements.   **(7 marks)**

```
Enter a word: homer
HOMER
Enter a word: MARGE
marge
Enter a word: Bart
Try again.
Enter a word:
Goodbye
```

> The function **len()** can be used to find an empty string.

Input and output

User **input** is provided via the keyboard. Program **outputs** are normally displayed on the screen. All outputs should be **fit for purpose** and suitable for the intended **audience**.

Keyboard input

Each key pressed on the keyboard generates a character. The input() function is used to capture these characters. The input() function always returns a string data type.

```
1   aString = input ("Name: ")
2   anInteger = int (input ("Integer: "))
3   aReal = float (input ("Decimal: "))
```

Remember you must convert the string input to the data type you need.

Display output

Use the print() function to display variables of any data type to the user's screen.

Use the conversion function, str(), and concatenation, +, to produce better formatted outputs.

```
1   print (aString, aReal)
2   print (aString + str (aReal))
```

Using a comma to separate items displays extra spaces.

Concatenation joins two strings, so use the str() function to convert any other data type to a string.

Columnar output

Use the <string>.format() function to create customised outputs, including tables.

```
1    letters = ["A", "B"]
2    column1 = [1, 2]
3    column2 = [10.5, 20.90]
4    layout = "{:<7}  {:^5}  {:^5}"
5    print (layout.format ("Letters",
6                          "Col 1", "Col 2"))
7    print ("-" * 22)
8    layout = "{:^7}  {:^5}  {:>5.2f}"
9    for index in range (len (letters)):
10       print (layout.format (letters[index],
11                             column1[index],
12                             column2[index]))
```

Use the positional parameters, { }, to provide spacings. The <, ^ and > symbols show alignment. The numbers show spacing widths.

Use the multiplication symbol to print a character many times.

Use a decimal and 'f' to show fractional numbers.

Remember that column headers may need a different format from the one used for column contents.

The code displays this table:

Letters	Col 1	Col 2
A	1	10.50
B	2	20.90

Now try this

Target grade **1-3**

A program must meet these requirements:

- accept a user's name
- greet the user with 'Hello' and name, using string concatenation
- accept an integer number and a decimal number

- calculate the mean of the numbers using addition and division
- display the mean to three decimal places, using <string>.format().

Write the program.

(10 marks)

Read files

Data that is stored on external storage media must be read into memory before a program can manipulate it.

Text files

The text files you will work with in your exam are all stored as character strings. Each record is one single string. Each field in the record is separated by a comma. Each record in the file is on a separate line.

Carriage return and line feed

Although you don't see them, there are one or more non-printable characters at the end of each line. These are carriage return and line feed.

If you open a text file in an editor, it will look like this example (which is a text file of prizes).

> Teddy Bear,2215,4.25
>
> Goldfish,2977,1.07
>
> Inflatable Hammer,1785,1.49
>
> Jumbo Sunglasses,1931,3.18

There are no spaces after the commas. There is no comma after the last field in each record.

Reading a file

Code is needed to read data from a text file and to store that data in the right data structure within a program.

```
1    prizeTable = []
2
3    file = open ("Prizes.txt", "r")
4    for line in file:
5        line = line.strip ()
6
7        fields = line.split (",")
8
9        prize = []
10
11       prize.append (fields[0])
12       prize.append (int (fields[1]))
13       prize.append (float (fields[2]))
14
15       prizeTable.append (prize)
16
17   file.close ()
```

Open the file in read mode, using 'r'.

Use iteration to access each line in the file in turn.

Strip off the line feed at the end of the line.

Split the line on the comma into separate fields and store in a list.

The content of the fields should be stored in a data type suitable for the problem. Lines 11 to 13 show the conversions.

Always remember to close your files.

Now try this

Target grade 7-9

Create a file, named 'Cars.txt'. Type the makes, models, years and prices from the box into the file. Make sure you copy the lines exactly. Save the file.

A program is required to:

- read the data from the 'Cars.txt' file into a two-dimensional data structure
- display all fields of each record of the two-dimensional data structure on a single line.

Write a program to meet these requirements.   **(10 marks)**

> CarA,ModelA,2011,5890.77
>
> CarB,ModelB,2010,8950.23
>
> CarC,ModelC,2009,5750.5
>
> CarD,ModelD,2009,16000
>
> CarE,ModelE,2014,5999.99

Write files

Data only exists in memory as long as the program is running. If the data is needed again, it must be saved. The data in the internal data structures should be saved to a file on a secondary storage device. The data is saved by writing it to a file. It is good practice to write data to a file before the program completes.

Text files

The text files you write as part of your exam will be of the same format as the text files you read. Each record is one single string. Each field in the record is separated by a comma. Each record in the file is on a separate line.

Line feed

You will need to add a line feed character to each of your output lines. Without the line feed character, all the characters in the file would be on one very long line. Remember, you won't see the line feed in an editor.

If you open a text file in an editor, it will look like this:

Teddy Bear,2215,4.25
Goldfish,2977,1.07
Inflatable Hammer,1785,1.49
Jumbo Sunglasses,1931,3.18

There are no spaces after the commas. There is no comma after the last field in each record.

Writing a file

In the exam, the records you write will be stored in an internal data structure or constructed by the program. In order to write the code to store data in a file you need to do the following:

```
1   prizeTable = [
2       ["Teddy Bear", 2215, 4.25],
3       ["Goldfish", 2977, 1.07],
4       ["Barrel of Slime", 2448, 1.03]]
5   outLine = ""
6
7   file = open ("Prizes.txt", "w")
8   for prize in prizeTable:
9       outLine = prize[0] + ","
10      outLine = outLine + \
11              str (prize[1]) + ","
12      outLine = outLine + \
13              str (prize[2])
14      outLine = outLine + "\n"
15      file.write (outLine)
16  file.close ()
```

Open the file in write mode.

Use iteration through all the items in the data structure, building one record at a time.

Convert every field to a string and concatenate them together, adding a comma between fields.

Add the line feed last.

Write the line you have just created.

Always close an open file.

Write mode will create a file if it does not exist and delete the contents of an existing file.

Now try this

Target grade 7-9

A program holds records about cars in an internal data structure. Here is the data structure.

```
carTable = [["Renault", "Megan", 2011, 5890.77],
            ["Saab", "Vector Sport", 2010, 8950.23],
            ["BMW", "Series 2.0", 2009, 5750.53],
            ["Honda", "Roadster", 2009, 16000],
            ["Vauxhall", "Cascada", 2014, 5999.99]]
```

A program is required to store the contents of the data structure in a text file, with each record on one line and each field separated by a comma.

Write a program to meet these requirements.

(10 marks)

Problem-solving
with programming

Validation

Validation ensures that program **input is fit for processing**. Programmers must not let 'garbage' into their programs or they will get 'garbage' out. Validation uses a number of different types of check.

Length check

You use this type of check to make sure the user has provided an input that is the correct length to be processed.

Use the len() function and a relational operator to check the length

```
1   key = "0000"
2   key = input ("Enter key: ")
3   if (len (key) != 4):
4       print ("Invalid length")
5   else:
6       print ("Good key")
```

Presence check

You must check to ensure the user has provided any input at all.

Use the len() function and check to see if the length is zero.

You can also compare against an empty string.

Entering nothing is a good way to stop a loop from executing.

```
1   key = "0000"
2   key = input ("Enter key: ")
3
4   if (len (key) == 0):
5       print ("Must enter key")
6
7   if (key == ""):
8       print ("Empty not allowed")
```

Range check

This type of check sees if a value falls between two bounds. This works with both numeric and string values.

```
1    age = 0
2    letter = ""
3
4    age = int (input ("Age: "))
5    if ((age < 1) or (age > 110)):
6        print ("Invalid age")
7
8    letter = input ("Letter: ")
9    letter = letter.upper ()
10   if ((letter > "A") and (letter <= "Z")):
11       print ("Good letter")
```

Use a relational operator for each bound with a Boolean operator in between. The check can indicate valid or invalid, depending on the operators. The checks here are for invalid input.

In this example, the code checks that the user's age is between 1 and 110, and that the letter entered exists in the upper-case alphabet.

Now try this

Target grade **4-6**

A program must report whether the following user inputs are valid or invalid, based on the given criteria:

- **User's name**: at least three characters long; no more than 20 characters in length.
- **Pizza toppings**: Between zero and eight, inclusive.
- **Letter grade**: A, B, C, D, E or F only.
- **The roll of two dice**: A valid number.

Use relational operators with Boolean operators to make your tests.

'Exit' should be printed if the user enters nothing to a prompt.

Write a program to meet these requirements.   **(10 marks)**

Pattern check

A pattern check is a type of validation that ensures data exactly matches a specified design so that it is fit for processing.

Approach

Each pattern check requires a different solution. To create that solution, you will need to use all the string manipulation subprograms that you know about.

Pattern matching

Programming languages have special techniques for pattern matching, but you do not need to learn these. Use what you already know.

Worked example

Target grade **7-9**

A national identity (ID) number has the format of 'LL DD DD', where 'L' represents a letter (any case) and 'D' represents a digit from 0 to 9. The ID number is entered by the user and needs validation with a pattern check. Error messages should be informative and specific to the error found.

Write a program to meet these requirements.   **(7 marks)**

> Initialising the input to a valid pattern will help you remember the rules as you write the code.

Sample answer

```
1    SPACE = " "
2    theNum = "QQ 12 34"
3    digits = ""
4
5    theNum = input ("ID number: ")
6
7    if (len (theNum) == 8):
8        if (theNum[0].isalpha() and theNum[1].isalpha()):
9            for index in range (3, 5):
10               digits = digits + theNum[index]
11           for index in range (6, 8):
12               digits = digits + theNum[index]
13           if (digits.isdigit()):
14               if ((theNum[2] == SPACE) and
15                       (theNum[5] == SPACE)):
16                   print ("Valid number")
17               else:
18                   print ("Spaces not right")
19           else:
20               print ("Digits not right")
21       else:
22           print ("Letters not right")
23   else:
24       print ("Length error")
```

Use len() to check for overall length.

Use <string>.isalpha()to check for letters in the right positions.

Copy out the digits into a variable.

Use <string>.isdigit() to make sure they are all 0 to 9.

Use indexing to check that the space characters are in the right place.

Now try this

Target grade **4-6**

A program must validate a key entered by the user. The format of the key is 'LDD', where 'L' represents a letter (any case) and 'D' represents a digit from 0 to 9. Error messages should be informative and specific to the error found. The program should work for all anticipated inputs.

Write a program to meet these requirements.   **(7 marks)**

Authentication

Authentication is used to ensure that a person attempting to log into a computer system or device is **permitted** to have access. Most systems use a username and a password for this.

Data structures

Usernames and passwords are most often stored in database tables.

 Links You can find out more about tables on page 82 and linear searching on page 15.

A table can be represented by a two-dimensional data structure, implemented as a list. Each record holds information about an individual user. Although authentication involves usernames and passwords, the program logic is the same as an **efficient linear search**.

Worked example

Target grade 7-9

A program must authenticate a username and password entered by the user. Valid user names and passwords are stored in a two-dimensional data structure in the top of the code file. Write a program to authenticate a username and passcode. **(7 marks)**

Sample answer

```
1   userTable = [["PHU9015", "stripes"],
2                ["PCG9951", "polkadots"],
3                ["VBS9395", "squiggles"]]
4   userName = ""
5   password = ""
6   found = False
7   index = 0
8   user = []
9
10  userName = input ("Enter user name: ")
11  password = input ("Enter password: ")
12
13  while ((index < len (userTable)) and
14        (not found)):
15     user = userTable[index]
16     if ((user[0] == userName) and
17        (user[1] == password)):
18        found = True
19     else:
20        index = index + 1
21
22  if (found):
23     print ("You're allowed in")
24  else:
25     print ("Invalid login")
```

The data structure holds the username in the first column and the password in the second column.

This loop continues as long as there are more users to look at and the entered data is not found.

Remember, the `len()` function only works on strings or lists, not on numbers.

Notice that both pieces of information must match to give access.

Using a variable to flag 'when found' means the loop can stop without having to look at all the records in the table.

Now try this

Target grade 7-9

A program must validate a username and passcode entered by the user. The passcode must be four digits long. It has been stored as an integer. Here is the data stored in the user table.

```
userTable = [["AAA34", 4860], ["CAB98", 7101], ["GUS21", 5975]]
```

Write a program to authenticate a username and passcode. **(10 marks)**

Problem-solving with programming

Arithmetic operators

Arithmetic operators are used to perform all basic calculations.

Links You can find out more about arithmetic operators on page 10.

Symbols

The arithmetic operators you need to know are:

Operator	Function
+	Addition
-	Subtraction
*	Multiplication
/	Division
%	Modulus
//	Integer division
**	Exponentiation

Data types

The data type of the result of an arithmetic expression depends on the data type of the initial operands.

- Division always returns a real number, even if the operands are integers.
- Multiplication of a string and an integer generates repeated characters.
- The addition symbol between two strings is concatenation.

BIDMAS

Python follows the BIDMAS order of precedence:

Brackets

Indices or powers

Division (division, modulus and integer division)

Multiplication

Addition

Subtraction

Using arithmetic operators

Look at this program. It applies each of the arithmetic operators to the numbers 7 and 4 and prints the answer.

This will always generate a real number.

On this line, num1 is raised to the power of num2.

The output of the program is below.

```
Add 7 4 11
Subtract 7 4 3
Multiply 7 4 28
Divide 7 4 1.75
Exponentiation 7 4 2401
Modulus 7 4 3
Integer Division 7 4 1
==========
Hello World
```

Modulus is the remainder after num1 ÷ num2.

Integer division is the whole number part of the quotient after num1 ÷ num2.

```
1   num1 = 7
2   num2 = 4
3
4   print ("Add", num1, num2, num1 + num2)
5   print ("Subtract", num1, num2,
6          num1 - num2)
7   print ("Multiply", num1, num2,
8          num1 * num2)
9   print ("Divide", num1, num2,
10         num1 / num2)
11
12  print ("Exponentiation", num1, num2,
13         num1 ** num2)
14  print ("Modulus", num1, num2,
15         num1 % num2)
16  print ("Integer Division", num1, num2,
17         num1 // num2)
18
19  print ("=" * 10)
20  print ("Hello" + " World")
```

Now try this

Target grade 4-6

A program is required to calculate the volume and surface area of a sphere, to three decimal places. The formulas for these calculations are shown here, where r is the radius – an integer value entered by the user.

- Volume = $(4/3) \times \pi \times r^3$
- Surface area = $4 \times \pi \times r^2$

Write a program to meet the stated requirements. **(10 marks)**

Remember that to use pi (π) you will need to import the math library.

Problem-solving with programming

Relational operators

Relational operators allow programmers to write programs that make decisions.

Symbols

The relational operators are:

Symbol	Meaning
< , <=	Less than, less than or equal
> , >=	Greater than, greater than or equal
== , !=	Equal, not equal

 Links   You can find out more about relational operators on page 10.

Relational operators and strings

Relational operators can be used with characters and strings as well as numbers. Strings are treated as their ASCII code equivalent number value. This gives an order for all characters as 0–9, A–Z, a–z.

 Links   You can find out more about ASCII on page 28.

Using relational operators

Relational operators are used with **selection** (**if…elif…else**) and **repetition** (**while**) to run tests. The flow of the execution of a program depends on the outcome of the tests.

In this example, the program prints responses based on the outcomes produced by a variety of relational operators. It uses selection and then repetition.

The output is shown below.

```
False
Below 50
Not H
Above 33.333
0
1
2
```

This instruction uses a Boolean value in selection.

Each part of the selection can include a different test using a relational operator.

Characters and strings can be tested directly.

This instruction uses a relational operator in repetition to keep the loop going around several times.

```
1   count = 31
2   letter = "Q"
3   name = ""
4   real = 33.334
5   myBoolean = False
6
7   if (myBoolean == False):
8       print ("False")
9
10  if (count < 50):
11      print ("Below 50")
12  elif (count > 100):
13      print ("Above 100")
14
15  if (letter != "H"):
16      print ("Not H")
17
18  if (real > 33.333):
19      print ("Above 33.333")
20
21  count = 0
22  while (count <= 2):
23      print (count)
24      count = count + 1
```

Now try this

Target grade 4-6

A program is required to determine the alphabetical order of strings. The user inputs the number of times that the program should loop. The user enters two strings on each pass of the loop. The program determines if the first string is equal to, less than, or greater than the second string.

Write a program to meet these requirements.

(7 marks)

Logical operators

Logical operators, used with relational operators, allow programmers to write programs that make decisions in groups. Logical operators are sometimes called Boolean operators.

Symbols

The logical operators are:

Symbol	Meaning
and	Both sides must be true to return true
or	Either side must be true to return true
not	Inverts the result

 Links   You can find out more about logical operators on page 11.

Data types

The inputs to the logical operators can only themselves be Boolean. The input(s) to a logical operator are first evaluated to find out if its result is 'true' or 'false'. The result(s) of this evaluation is then fed into the logical operator to get a final result.

> The 'and' and 'or' operators need an argument on both sides. The 'not' operator only needs one argument, on the right side.

Using logical operators

Logical operators are used with **selection** (**if…elif…else**) and **repetition** (**while**) to run test conditions. The flow of the execution of a program depends on the outcome of all the tests.

This example program shows each logical operator, but is not a solution to a problem.

It produces the output shown in the box.

```
Invalid
Safe to enter
Stay out
1
2
3
4
```

Each side of the 'or' will evaluate to true or false.

Both sides of the 'and' must be true to return true.

Using 'not' inverts the test, so false becomes true and true becomes false.

The repetition in this line uses 'not', but it can also use 'and' and 'or' (just as in the other lines).

```
1    roll = 7
2    guess = -2
3    total = 0
4    count = 4
5    statElectricity = False
6    statWater = True
7
8    if ((roll > 6) or (guess < 1)):
9        print ("Invalid")
10
11   if ((statWater == True) and
12       (statElectricity == False)):
13       print ("Safe to enter")
14
15   statElectricity = True
16   if ((statWater) and
17       (not statElectricity)):
18       print ("Safe to enter")
19   else:
20       print ("Stay out")
21
22   while (not (total >= 4)):
23       total = total + 1
24       print (total)
```

Now try this

Target grade 4-6

A 'guess the number' program is being written.

The target is between 1 and 10. The input number must be validated to be between 1 and 10.

The program allows for three guesses. It prints 'Well Done!!' if the target number is guessed correctly and 'Better luck next time' if it is not guessed.

The program has the following variables already declared:

```
guessed = False
count = 0
target = 2
num = 0
```

Write a program to use these variables and meet the stated requirements. **(10 marks)**

Subprograms

A subprogram is a self-contained sequence of program instructions that performs a specific task. On this page, you will revise how to use built-in subprograms and subprograms stored in libraries.

 Links   You can find out more about subprograms on page 2.

Facts about subprograms

☑ A **function** is a subprogram that returns a value to the main program when it is called.

☑ A **procedure** is a subprogram that does not return a value to the main program.

☑ Values passed to the subprogram from the calling code are **arguments**.

☑ The arguments are copied to a subprogram's **parameters**, the placeholders in the subprogram's definition.

Built-in subprograms

Many subprograms are provided in Python and are accessible from everywhere in your programs. They perform commonly used tasks, such as printing, finding the length, taking input and converting between data types.

```
1    name = ""
2    length = 0
3    decimal = 0.0
4
5    name = input ("Name: ")
6    length = len (name)
7    print (name, length)
8
9    decimal = float (input ("Decimal : "))
10   decimal = round (decimal, 2)
11   print (decimal)
```

The function input() is built-in and returns a string value.

len() is also a built-in function. It returns an integer value.

print() is a built-in procedure. It does not return a value to the caller when it finishes.

float() and round() are built-in functions that return values with decimals.

Library subprograms

Subprograms that perform related tasks are grouped together in libraries. To use these, you have to import the library into your program. Common libraries are 'time', 'random', 'math' and 'turtle' graphics.

This example code demonstrates the use of library functions and constants.

```
1    import random
2    import math
3
4    roll = 0
5    decimal = 0.0
6
7    roll = random.randint (1, 6)
8    print (roll)
9    decimal = random.random ()
10   print (decimal)
11
12   print (math.pi)
```

Use the keyword import followed by the name of a library to gain access to subprograms in that library.

To call a library subprogram, prefix the subprogram call with the name of the library.

random() is a function in the random library that returns a decimal value.

Now try this

Write a program to:
- generate two random real numbers
- multiply the first by 1000
- multiply the second by 10
- generate a third number by multiplying the first two
- print the third number rounded to four decimal places
- print the floor of the third number
- print the ceiling of the third number. **(10 marks)**

 The floor of a real number is the largest integer less than or equal to the original. The ceiling of a real number is the smallest integer greater than or equal to the original. You can find these functions in the math library.

Functions

A function is a type of subprogram that **returns a value** to the calling code. You can create your own functions to perform specific tasks.

Creating a function

The following code shows a function to calculate the velocity of an object.

To create a subprogram, you need to define it with the keyword def.

velocity is a local variable as it is accessible only within the subprogram and not in the main program.

```
5    def calcVelocity (pDistance, pTime):
6        velocity = 0.0
7        velocity = pDistance / pTime
8        return (velocity)
```

pDistance and pTime are parameters that store the values sent from the main program in the subprogram.

A result is returned to the main program, so this subprogram is a function.

This is the same function that is called in the code below.

Naming parameters

Starting parameter names with 'p' is good practice, as you will not get into a muddle with other variable names.

Calling a function

Functions can be called from the main program or from other subprograms. In the code below, the calcVelocity() function is called to calculate the velocity from the user's input.

❶

The right side of this = symbol calls the subprogram and passes the global variables (distance, time) to it as arguments in the correct order.

❸

The assignment catches the returned value from the function into a variable.

```
1    avgVelocity = 0.0
2    distance = 0.0
3    time = 0.0
4
5    def calcVelocity (pDistance, pTime):
6        velocity = 0.0
7        velocity = pDistance / pTime
8        return (velocity)
9
10   distance = float (input ("Distance: "))
11   time = float (input ("Time: "))
12   avgVelocity = calcVelocity (distance, time)
13   print (avgVelocity)
```

❷

The values in the arguments are copied into the parameters 'pDistance' and 'pTime'.

Remember, values passed into the call to a subprogram are named 'arguments', while the values holding the passed in values inside the subprogram are called 'parameters'.

Now try this

Target grade **4-6**

A program is required to calculate the area of a rectangle.
The program must:

* accept the length and width of the rectangle from the user
* use a subprogram, with two parameters, to calculate the area
* return the area to the main program
* display the area.

Write a program to meet these requirements.   **(10 marks)**

Remember to name your parameters so they are not confused with the variables in your main program.

Procedures

A procedure is a type of subprogram that performs a task, but **does not return a value** to the calling code. You can create your own procedures to perform specific tasks.

Creating a procedure

The following code shows a procedure to display a simple menu.

To create a subprogram, you need to define it with the keyword def.

There is no return keyword used here, so this subprogram is a procedure.

This procedure is the same one used in the code below.

```
3    def showMenu (pType):
4        if (pType == "N"):
5            print ("1 – Search")
6            print ("2 – Delete")
7            print ("3 – Add")
8        else:
9            print ("A – Search")
10            print ("B – Delete")
11            print ("C – Add")
```

pType is a parameter that stores the value sent from the main program into the subprogram.

Remember, starting parameter names with 'p' is good practice, as you will not get into a muddle with other variable names.

Calling a procedure

Procedures can be called from the main program or from other subprograms. This code asks the user to choose between two different menus (numbers or letters). The procedure displays the chosen menu type.

```
1    typeMenu = ""
2
3    def showMenu (pType):
4        if (pType == "N"):
5            print ("1 – Search")
6            print ("2 – Delete")
7            print ("3 – Add")
8        else:
9            print ("A – Search")
10            print ("B – Delete")
11            print ("C – Add")
12
13    typeMenu = input ("N for number: ")
14    typeMenu = typeMenu.upper()
15    showMenu (typeMenu)
```

❶ This line calls the subprogram and passes the global variable (typeMenu) to it as an argument.

❸ Notice that there is no code to catch a return value. The calling code recognises that the subprogram is a procedure.

❷ The value in the argument is copied into the parameter pType.

Now try this

Target grade 1-3

A program is required to use turtle graphics to draw a square on the screen.
The program must:

- use a procedure to draw the square
- take four input parameters to the procedure (the turtle, x-position, y-position and length of side)
- use `<turtle>.penup()` and `<turtle>.pendown()` to stop drawing during positioning
- use a loop to draw the sides
- function correctly for all anticipated input.

Write a program to meet these requirements.

(10 marks)

Local and global variables

The term **scope** means the area of a program in which a variable is accessible. Variables exist and are accessible in the scope where they are first created. Variables are either created in local scope or global scope. Different variables can have exactly the same name because they exist in different scopes. The variables will reside in different locations in RAM. Their names may be the same, but their contents will be different.

Local scope and local variables

- Local scope describes only a single subprogram.
- Local variables are only accessible in local scope (i.e. the subprogram in which they are created).

Global scope and global variables

- Global scope describes the entire executing program.
- Global variables are accessible from the main program and all subprograms.

Using global and local variables

```
1    # ----- Global Variables -----
2    theNumbers = [1, 2, 3, 4, 5]
3    total = 154
4    # ----- Subprograms -----
5    def doAvg (pNums):
6        avg = 0.0
7        total = 0
8        for number in pNums:
9            total = total + number
10       avg = total / len (pNums)
11       return (avg)
12   # ----- Main Program -----
13   print (doAvg (theNumbers))
14   print (total)
```

This variable total is at global scope, accessible from anywhere in the executing program.

This variable total is at local scope, accessible from this subprogram, doAvg(), only.

When a variable name is encountered, such as total on line 9, the variable value is chosen from the nearest scope. In this case, the local variable used is the one from line 7.

Local scope is always checked first to find the variable, before going to global scope.

Now try this

Target grade 4-6

In this program there is a local variable named 'answer' and a global variable named 'answer'.

1 Give a line number where the local variable 'answer' is used. **(1 mark)**

2 Give a line number where the global variable 'answer' is used. **(1 mark)**

```
1    # ----- Global Variables -----
2    base = 15
3    height = 14
4    answer = 73
5    # ----- Subprograms -----
6    def calcArea (pBase, pHeight):
7        answer = 0.0
8        print (answer)
9        answer = (1/2) * pBase * pHeight
10       return (answer)
11   # ----- Main Program -----
12   print (answer)
13   answer = calcArea (base, height)
14   print (answer)
```

Answers

1. Decomposition and abstraction

1 Your definition could include the following:
   - The processes of removing unnecessary detail so that only the most important points remain.
   - The process of focusing on what is important and ignoring anything that is not important.

2 Your answer could include the following:
   - To reduce the size of the problem.
   - To share out the different parts of the problem to different people.

2. Using subprograms

Your answer could include the following:

- Subprograms make code easier to design, code and debug because they break down a complex program into a number of smaller, less complicated parts.
- Subprograms make the logic of code clearer because you can replace blocks of code with calls to subprograms that have meaningful names.
- Subprograms make it easier to maintain code because subprograms can be modified or changed without affecting the rest of the program.
- Subprograms avoid unnecessary duplication of code because they can be used as many times as needed within a program.

3. Algorithms: flowcharts

Your flowchart should contain the following:

- A start and stop symbol.
- A process symbol for the creation of a variable.
- An input symbol and taking variable 'name' from keyboard.
- An output symbol that shows "Hello" with variable. (Ignore use of concatenation or comma.)
- Use of arrows to connect all symbols in sequence.

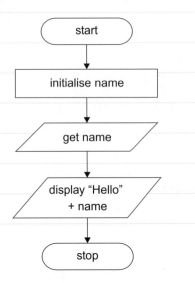

4. Algorithms: selection

1 Large
2 Small
3 Medium
4 Medium

5. Algorithms: repetition

1 Loops use the existing selection symbol because one output can be a backward pointing arrow to the top of the selection.

2 Could be one of: While, Until, As long as.

6. Algorithms: iteration

1 Your definition could include:
   - The process of looping through every item in a data structure/list.
   - Repeating a set of instructions for every item in a data structure/list.

2 A data structure/list/string. A backward pointing arrow to a selection/if symbol.

7. Variables and constants

Remember, suitable variable names make it clear what data the variable will hold.

Suitable variables could be: result1, result2, result3, result4, result5, total, theMean.

8. Arrays

Your algorithm should include:

1 Get the firstName and the lastName from the user.

2 Assume found is false, because the target is not seen yet.

3 Point to the first row in the array of friends by using an index of 0.

4 Loop through the friends.

5 Check if found yet, if so, then go to step 8.

6 Check if there are any more friends to look at by checking value of index, if no more, then go to step 8.

7 Check if friends[index][0] is equal to the firstName and if friends[index][1] is equal to the lastName, if so, then set found to true, then go to step 4, otherwise, point to next friend by adding one to index and go back to step 4.

8 Check how we got out of the loop.

9 If found is true, then print "Found the friend", otherwise we ran out of friends, so print "Friend is not in the array".

9. Records

1 and 2

Description	Code	Stock	Price
"Book"	6644	17	27.45
"Poster"	876	67	10.00	⟵ Record
"DVD"	7465	135	7.35
"Book"	957	212	5.50

Field

3 16
4 [1][3]

10. Arithmetic and relational operators

Modulus returns the remainder after division, whereas integer division returns the quotient/integer part after division.

11. Logical operators

Met

12. Determining correct output

number	index	output
3		
3	0	3
4	1	4
6	2	6

13. Using trace tables

result	total	thePower	output
0	0		
1	1	0	1
2	3	1	2
4	7	2	4
8	15	3	8
			15

14. Errors that can occur in programs

The logic of an algorithm may be incorrect, causing it to produce an incorrect or unexpected result.

15. Linear search

- Finding the target item.
- Reaching the end of the list.

16. Binary search

- **Step 1**: The median item is 27 but this is higher than the search item.
- **Step 2**: The sub-list to the left is used: 3, 5, 9, 14, 17, 21.
- **Step 3**: The median is 9 but this is too low. The sub-list 14, 17, 21 is used.
- **Step 4**: The median selected is 17 which is the search item.

17. Bubble sort

The items that have been moved are shown in red. You will not need to do this in the exam.

Pass 1	Pass 2
4 1 2 6 3 5	1 2 4 3 5 6
1 4 2 6 3 5	1 2 3 4 5 6
1 2 4 6 3 5	1 2 3 4 5 6
1 2 4 6 3 5	
1 2 4 3 6 5	
1 2 4 3 5 6	

18. Merge sort

| 38 | 27 | 43 | 3 | 9 | 82 | 10 |

| 38 | 27 | 43 | 3 | 9 | 82 | 10 |

| 38 | 27 | 43 | 3 | 9 | 82 | 10 |

| 38 | 27 | 43 | 3 | 9 | 82 | 10 |

| 27 | 38 | 3 | 43 | 9 | 82 | 10 |

| 3 | 27 | 38 | 43 | 9 | 10 | 82 |

| 3 | 9 | 10 | 27 | 38 | 43 | 82 |

19. Efficiency of algorithms

- **Stage 1**:
  The median item is 'Mateo' but this is a higher value than the search item.
- **Stage 2**:
  The sublist to the left is selected: Ahmad, Ava, Emma, Josiah.
- **Stage 3**:
  The median for this list is 'Ava', which is the search item.

20. Logical operators

1   P = A AND NOT B

2   There are different table representations

A	B	P
0	0	0
0	1	0
1	0	1
1	1	0

21. Using binary

The microprocessor hardware only operates on bits and so has no concept of type or representation.

22. Unsigned integers

1   1 1 0 0 1 0 1 1
    1 1 1 1 0 0 0 1
    0 1 0 0 1 1 1 1
    0 1 1 0 0 1 0 0

2   $(1 \times 128) + (1 \times 64) + (1 \times 16) + (1 \times 8) + (1 \times 1)$
    = 217

23. Two's complement signed integers

+9	0	0	0	0	1	0	0	1
−9	1	1	1	1	0	1	1	1

24. Binary addition

1 1 0 0 1 1 1 0

25. Logical and arithmetic shifts

1   0 1 0 1 0 0 0 0
2   0 0 0 1 0 1 1 1
3   1 1 0 0 0 1 0 0

26. Overflow

1   The registers inside the machine that hold the original patterns are fixed in width, and so no more than 16 bits can be held.

2   1 0 1 0 1 1 0 1

27. Hexadecimal

```
          E9
    14              9
    1110          1001
        1110 1001
```

28. Characters

77

29. Bitmap images

Your answer could include the following points:

*   The quality of the image is affected by the number of pixels that make it up. Therefore, the more pixels the better the image resolution.
*   The quality of the image is affected by the number of bits used to encode the colour of each pixel/colour depth, therefore, if more bits are used, more colours can be displayed.

30. Analogue sound

1   A digital recording samples the analogue signal at fixed intervals called the sampling frequency. Therefore the entire analogue signal is not represented in the digital recording.

2   $(44\,100 \times 16 \times 150 \times 2) \div (8 \times 1024 \times 1024)$ mebibytes

31. Limits of binary data representation

Five bits are needed to store 24 colours because $2^4 = 16$, which is less than 24, and $2^5 = 32$, which is the next largest power of 2 greater than 24.

32. Binary units of measurement

Divide the file size in mebibytes by 1024:
4096 / 1024.

33. Data compression

1   Compressing files reduces the file size for transmission, so that download times will be shorter/internet traffic will be reduced.

2   The best type of compression would be lossless, because a Python program would have to be reconstructed exactly to match the original or it would not work.

34. The stored program concept

Program instructions and data are stored in main memory and transferred/fetched one at a time to the CPU, where they are decoded and executed. Results of operations carried out in the CPU are stored in/written to memory.

35. The central processing unit (CPU)

The CPU needs to be able to read program instructions and data from memory and write the results of operations to memory.

36. The fetch-decode-execute cycle

Instructions are fetched from memory into the CPU sequentially/one at a time, where they are decoded and executed by the CU. Arithmetic and logic operations are performed by the ALU.

37. The need for secondary storage

Volatile storage is dependent on a constant power supply in order to retain its contents, whereas non-volatile storage retains its contents even when the power is turned off.

38. Types of secondary storage

Your answer might include:
- High capacity.
- Relatively cheap per unit of storage.
- Fast data access/retrieval.
- Can be kept off-site/away from the office.

39. Embedded systems

It uses a sensor to monitor the temperature of the water and turns the heating element on or off to maintain the correct temperature.

40. Operating system 1

The operating system shares out CPU time between processes, so that each process gets a share of CPU time/time slice. Processes are prioritised, so that those designated as high priority get more processor time/time slots than others.

41. Operating system 2

1 Files are organised in a hierarchy/tree structure. The top node is the root. A node is either a directory, a sub-directory or a file.
2 The OS maintains a record containing the start location and sequence number of each file block. It uses this to retrieve all the blocks belonging to the file. It puts the file blocks into the correct order to reconstruct the file.

42. Utility software

File compression software, because it would make the file quicker to upload.

43. Robust software

A quick fix solution may have unintended consequences in other areas of the program, because it is an unplanned change and is not rigorously tested, and so could affect the integrity of other parts of the software.

44. Programming languages

Using a low-level language ensures that the system's memory is used efficiently, because it enables the programmer to select the most appropriate instructions to use and to directly control the hardware to be used.

45. Interpreters and compilers

1 The compiler will optimise the code to make the most of the phone's limited resources, memory and power.
2 Esme will get immediate feedback. She will also be able to test and debug her program as she develops it.

46. Networks

1 A WAN is used because the company's stores are located over a wide geographical area in different towns and cities. A LAN only covers a small geographic area so would not be suitable for this purpose.
2 The technician can set up a remote access connection to the faulty device, enabling them to run diagnostic software to investigate and resolve the problem.

47. The internet

The web server should have a static IP address because it will always stay the same. This means that the DNS will have the correct IP address, enabling browsers to locate the web server.

48. Packet switching

The sequence number is used to reassemble data packets into the correct order, because data packets may be out of sequence on arrival.

The checksum is used for error checking. The receiving computer reapplies the checksum formula to the data in the packet and compares it with the one included in the header. If the two are not the same, it issues a resend request.

49. Wired versus wireless

Your answer might include three of the following:
- Fibre-optic cable provides more bandwidth than copper wire.
- Fibre-optic cable transmits data over longer distances than copper wire.
- Unlike copper wire, fibre-optic cable is immune to electrical interference.
- Fibre-optic cable presents less of a security risk than copper wire.

50. Connectivity on a LAN

A wired network has a higher bandwidth than a wireless network – this will prevent long delays in lessons while multimedia content downloads.

Transmissions on a wired network are difficult to intercept, which will help the school keep sensitive personal data relating to pupils and staff secure.

A wired network can reach further, which will enable all the buildings on the school site to be connected. There is also less likelihood of lessons being disrupted by transmission failure because, unlike a wireless transmission, walls and other electronic devices do not interfere with the wired signal.

If the school opts for a wireless network, students will be able to bring their own portable devices to school and log on to the network, obviating the need for the school to supply them all with laptops – though this would have security implications.

Lessons and other activities will not be disrupted while a wireless network is being installed because not much cable will need to be laid.

With a wireless network, students and teachers can remain connected to the network as they move from room to room because their portable devices do not have to be plugged in to a cable.

51. Network speeds

$((3.2 \times 1000 \times 1000 \times 1000) \div 8) \times 15$

52. Network protocols

The POP protocol deletes messages on the email server once they have been downloaded, whereas the IMAP protocol leaves the messages on the email server.

53. The TCP/IP model

The link layer converts the binary data received from the internet layer into electrical, light or radio signals for transmission across the network to the router.

54. Network topologies

A mesh network is more robust than a star network because it does not have a single point of failure. If one node fails, data is rerouted to avoid it, whereas, should the central node of a star network fail, the whole network will go down.

55. Network security

Penetration testing by a security expert will identify network vulnerabilities that a hacker could exploit to gain unauthorised access to the company's data, and provide advice on what to do to fix them.

56. Protecting networks

A firewall acts as a barrier between a network and the internet. It uses a pre-defined set of rules to determine which traffic is allowed in and out and which is blocked. This will prevent a hacker from gaining access to the network from outside. Should someone succeed in getting into the network in some other way, the firewall will block them from accessing websites to download malicious software.

57. Environmental issues 1

They need electricity to power their servers, and to keep them cool.

58. Environmental issues 2

Your answer might mention two of the following issues:
- They can be located in cold regions of the world, so it takes less energy to keep the storage devices cool.
- They can use a renewable source of energy, rather than fossil fuels.
- They can use natural cooling systems, e.g. piped water, instead of air conditioners.
- The heat produced by their servers can be used to heat homes and public buildings located close by.

59. Personal data

Trends and sub-group variations can be identified, thereby enabling governments to forecast future needs more accurately, and so make more informed decisions.

60. Legislation

In order to respond to new types of cybercrime, such as ransomware attacks and cyber terrorism.

61. Artificial intelligence (AI)

The algorithm might have been trained using historical data gathered at a time when almost all software developers were male.

62. Protecting intellectual property 1

- By registering the copyright, Mandeep can protect the source/object code of the app.
- By getting a patent granted, he will have exclusive rights to make, use and sell the app.

63. Protecting intellectual property 2

Your answer might mention two of the following:

- Open-source software is usually free to use, whereas a network licence for proprietary software would be expensive.
- Providing there is someone with sufficient technical skills, the school will be able to customise the software so that it will fully meet its needs.
- The school will be able to take advantage of the free support provided by the open-source community.

64. Threats to digital systems 1

Your answer might mention three of the following:

- It can cause a computer, network or website to run more slowly or crash.
- It can corrupt or destroy data.
- It can encrypt data so that it is inaccessible to users until a ransom is paid.
- It can lock users out of their account or
- computer.
- It can use up storage space leaving too little
- room for legitimate files.
- It can disrupt a person's workflow and concentration by displaying unwanted adverts.

65. Threats to digital systems 2

The virus may have gone undetected because it is so new that its signature has not yet been added to the anti-malware's signature library on Alex's laptop.

66. Threats to digital systems 3

Your answer might mention two of the following:

- To enable them to assume the victim's identity.
- To sell it on to a third party.
- To steal money from the victim's bank account.
- To extort money from the victim by threatening disclosure or locking them out of their account.

67. Protecting digital systems 1

Your answer might mention two of the following:

- The organisation should install and configure a firewall to prevent hackers from gaining unauthorised access to its network via the internet, and to control its employees' access to the internet from the network.
- Anti-malware software should be installed on every computer in order to detect and remove malware.
- All sensitive data should be encrypted, in order to protect its confidentiality in the event of it being stolen.

68. Protecting digital systems 2

1 It takes less time to complete, and takes up less storage capacity.

2 It is more time-consuming to restore the data, because this has to be done incrementally, starting from the last full backup and applying every subsequent incremental backup in sequence.

69. Decomposition and abstraction

Your answer code should include/do the following:

- Use of comments for decompositions, i.e. logic is set out and described in the comments.
- While loop stops for 0 input.
- For loop used with range to generate 12 numbers for table width.
- All output on a single line.
- Functions correctly.

 69 Decomposition and abstraction Model Answer.py

70. Read, analyse and refine programs

Your answer code should include/do the following:

- Numbers stored in a one-dimensional data structure implemented as a list.
- Processing of the data uses iteration, a for statement.
- Functions correctly, giving a result of 308.

 70 Read, analyse and refine programs Model Answer.py

71. Convert algorithms 1

Your answer code should include/do the following:
- Variable age initialised to 0.
- Variable total initialised to 0.0.
- Variable temperature initialised to 18.0.
- Accept age input.
- Conversion of age input to integer.
- Accept temperature input.
- Conversion of temperature input to float.
- Calculation of total by adding age and temperature.
- Using print() to display the total.
- Functions correctly for integer and real input.

 71 Convert algorithms 1 Model Answer.py

72. Convert algorithms 2

Your answer code should include/do the following:
- Variable name initialised to empty string.
- Accept name input.
- Conversion of name to upper case, using <string>.upper().
- Selection using if...else.
- Test with if uses string indexing for position [0].
- Output messages match correct test condition (i.e. last names less than J, sit in hall, otherwise sit in theatre).
- Functions correctly for any alphabetic string, upper or lower case.

 72 Convert algorithms 2 Model Answer.py

73. Convert algorithms 3

Your answer code should include/do the following:
- Variable choice initialised to empty string.
- Accept choice input.
- Repetition using while.
- Lookup check for "Y" or "y".
- Output messages meet requirement of flowchart.
- Functions correctly for "Y" or "y".
- Exits on any other alphabetic input.

 73 Convert algorithms 3 Model Answer.py

74. Convert algorithms 4

Your answer code should include/do the following:
- Use of for in range() loop.
- Use of –1 step in range().
- Use of –1 lower bound in range().

- Display of final message "Go!!".
- Functions correctly, i.e. prints 10...0.

 74 Convert algorithms 4 Model Answer.py

75. Convert algorithms 5

Your answer code should include/do the following:
- Import of random library.
- Initialisation of numList to empty list.
- Initialisation of total to 0.
- Count controlled loop (for in range/while) for generating 100 numbers.
- Random numbers must be between 100 and 500 (inclusive).
- Appending each random number to numList.
- Use of for ... in loop to process all numbers in the list.
- Adding each item in the list to the total.
- Display of final total.
- Functions correctly for a set of 100 integers.

 75 Convert algorithms 5 Model Answer.py

76. Readability

Your answer code should include/do the following:
- Labelled layout sections libraries, global variables and main program.
- Import of random placed at the top of the file.
- Variables have meaningful names in the context of the problem.
- Global variables initialised all together in one place.
- Use of white space to break up logic, such as processing (if...elif...else) distinct from inputs and outputs.
- Use of at least two comments to explain logic.
- Functions correctly for anticipated input.

 76 Readability Model Answer.py

77. Program errors

Your answer code should include/do the following:
- Syntax error (line 4) missing (before colours.
- Runtime error (line 6) replace equality operator == with assignment operator =.
- Logic error (line 2) initial value for index should be 0.

 77 Program errors Model Answer.py

78. Fitness for purpose and efficiency

Your answer code should include/do the following:

- Single print statement – reduces the chance of errors.
- if…elif…else instead of multiple if statements – reduces the number of executions.
- Order of tests either ascending or descending – reduces the need for compound tests.
- Fully functional for all anticipated input.

 78 Fitness for purpose and efficiency Model Answer.py

79. Structural components of programs

1 sideLength, tim, or numSides.
2 3, 4, or 6.
3 Any three numbers from 1 to 11 (except 2, 5 and 8) in order.
4 9 to 11.
5 You should answer with any one of the following parameter values:
- input() function – "Length: ".
- int() function – input ("Length: ").
- .pencolor() method – "BlueViolet".
- range() function – 4.
- .left() method – 90.

80. Iteration

Your answer code should include/do the following:

- Correct output going forward.
- Correct output of reversed even numbers only.
- Use of for each to print output going forward.
- Use of for in range to print output reversed, using a –2 step.
- Use of concatenation anywhere to join strings.
- Use of same output string in both loops, reset between.
- Functions correctly.

 80 Iteration Model Answer.py

81. Repetition

Your answer code should include/do the following:

- Four choices on the menu.
- Deal with both upper and lower case in any way.
- Keep user inside loop until valid input is entered.
- Print single message only for valid input.
- Use of Boolean operators to create compound test condition.
- Use of <string>.upper or <string>.lower to convert input to known state.
- Menu choices fit for purpose and suitable for the audience.

 81 Repetition Model Answer.py

82. Structured data types

Your answer code should include/do the following:

- Create and initialise a two-dimensional table of records for the paper information.
- All records contain a string, and two integers, in any order.
- Area for each paper size is calculated correctly (width * height).
- Name, width, length and area are displayed in columnar form using <string>.format().
- Area is displayed with two decimal places only.
- An iteration (for loop) is used instead of a repetition (while loop).
- Column names are fit for purpose.
- At least one comment is included to explain the logic.
- Code is laid out, including some white space, to ensure readability.
- Functions correctly for any number of paper sizes greater than one.

 82 Structured data types Model Answer.py

83. Data types, variables and constants

Your answer code should include/do the following:

- Up to four variables created in any way.
- Up to two constants, upper case, created any way.
- All six items have meaningful names.
- Up to three items created using separate declaration and initialisation.
- Up to three items created using implicit declaration and initialization.
- Program prints values for all six items, in any order or format.
- Program functions without errors.

Note: Values do not have to be accurate, only of the correct data type.

 83 Data types, variables and constants Model Answer.py

84. String manipulation

Your answer code should include/do the following:

- Accepts user input as string.
- Uses a while loop to identify exit condition.
- Use of the function len() to identify an empty string.
- Use of if…elif…else for checking case conditions.
- Use of <string>.isupper() to identify upper case.
- Use of <string>.lower() to convert upper case to lower case.
- Functions correctly for data shown in console session.

 84 String manipulation Model Answer.py

85. Input and output

Your answer code should include/do the following:

- Accept a user's name, using input().
- Greet the user with "Hello" and name, using concatenation.
- Accept an integer number, using conversion with int().
- Accept a real decimal number, using conversion with float().
- Display the two numbers on the same line using print().
- Calculation of mean includes addition of two numbers.
- Calculation of mean includes division by 2.
- Display the mean using <string>.format ().
- The placeholder in <string>.format() is correctly formed for three decimal places.
- Functions correctly for inputs of string, integer and real numbers.

 85 Input and output Model Answer.py

86. Read files

Your answer code should include/do the following:

- Opens the file in read mode.
- Uses a loop (for each, while not end of file) to read every line.
- Removes the line feed using <string>.strip().
- Separates the line into fields using <string>.split(",").
- Appends each field to a new record.
- Converts data types (int) and (float).
- Appends new record to data structure.
- File is closed before exiting the program.
- Output to screen is for individual fields, i.e. no []s.
- Functions correctly.

 86 Read files Model Answer.py

87. Write files

Your answer code should include/do the following:

- Opens the file in write mode.
- Uses a loop (for each, for in range) to iterate across the data structure.
- Appends two string fields to the output line.
- Appends integer field to output line, converting to string.
- Appends real field to output line, converting to string.
- Fields separated by commas.
- No spaces between fields in file.
- Appends line feed to output line.
- Writes the output line to the file.
- Closes the file.

 87 Write files Model Answer.py

88. Validation

Your answer code should include/do the following:

- Check for name uses len() function.
- Bounds on name are correct.
- Relational and Boolean operators for name check match.
- Relational and Boolean operators for toppings check match.
- Case of letter is controlled with <string>.upper() or <string>.lower().
- Relational and Boolean operators for letter check match.
- Bounds on roll are correct, i.e. 2,12 or 1,13.
- Relational and Boolean operators for roll check match.
- Presence check uses len()==0 or =="".
- All validation checks work for anticipated input.

 88 Validation Model Answer.py

89. Pattern check

Your answer code should include/do the following:

- Check for overall length using len().
- Check for alphabetic character using <string>.isalpha().
- Check for second character using <string>.isdigit().
- Check for third character using <string>.isdigit().
- Uses Boolean operator to implement both digit checks in one statement.
- Error messages are informative and specific.
- Pattern check works for anticipated input.

 89 Pattern check Model Answer.py

90. Authentication

Your answer code should include/do the following:

- Accepts passcode as string.
- Uses len() to check length of password.
- Converts password to integer.
- Use of while loop for searching userTable.
- Use of len() function with indexing to access each record.
- Use of Boolean flag to stop if found.
- Error messages are informative and precise.
- Functions correctly for record not there.
- Functions correctly for mismatched username and password.
- Functions correctly for found record.

 90 Authentication Model Answer.py

91. Arithmetic operators

Your answer code should include/do the following:

- Import math library.
- Accept input of radius from user.
- Convert radius to integer from string input.
- Volume:
  - Sight of 4/3.
  - Radius is raised to the power of 3.
  - Translation of formula completely accurate.
- Area:
  - Radius is raised to the power of 2.
  - Translation of formula completely accurate.
- Use of round() to round either/both results to three decimal places.
- Displays both results.

 91 Arithmetic operators Model Answer.py

92. Relational operators

Your answer code should include/do the following:

- Accept count from user.
- Convert count to integer.
- Use while or for in range to create a loop.
- Use selection if and relational operators for test conditions.
- Use if...elif...else instead of multiple if statements.
- Output messages match relational tests.
- Functions correctly for anticipated input.

 92 Relational operators Model Answer.py

93. Logical operators

Your answer code should include/do the following:

- Use while to create a loop.
- Loop uses guessed, and and count.
- Accept the guess from user.
- Convert the guess to an integer.
- Tests on validation use correct relational operators.
- Selection if for range check uses a Boolean operator.
- Selection if is used to check equal to target.
- Boolean guessed is set to true when match.
- Outputs match requirements.
- Functions correctly for anticipated input.

 93 Logical operators Model Answer.py

94. Subprograms

Your answer code should include/do the following:

- Import of random library.
- Import of math library.
- Use of random.random() to generate two numbers.
- Multiplication of first number by 1000.
- Multiplication of second number by 10.
- Multiplication of first number by second number.
- Use of round (<num>, 4).
- Use of math.floor (<num>).
- Use of math.ceil (<num>).
- Display of the results of round, floor and ceiling.

 94 Subprograms Model Answer.py

95. Functions

Your answer code should include/do the following:

- Length and width accepted from the keyboard.
- Length and width input converted to integer.
- Subprogram defined to calculate area has a meaningful name.
- Subprogram accepts two parameters, with meaningful names.
- Area is calculated by multiplication of two input parameters.
- Subprogram is called with two arguments.
- Calculated area is returned to the calling line.
- Returned calculated area is assigned to a variable in the calling line.
- Calculated area is displayed.
- Functions correctly for all anticipated input.

 95 Functions Model Answer.py

96. Procedures

Your answer code should include/do the following:

- Import of turtle library.
- Procedure defined to draw a square has meaningful name.
- Subprogram takes four parameters.
- Parameters are the turtle, x-position, y-position and length of side.
- Penup and pendown used to control drawing.
- Subprogram positions turtle to the value in the input parameters.

- for or while used to draw the square image.
- forward and left/right/setheading used to draw sides.
- Subprogram called with arguments to match parameters.
- Functions properly for all anticipated input.

 96 Procedures Model Answer.py

97. Local and global variables

1   7, 8, 9 or 10.
2   4, 12, 13 or 14.